# Proclaiming the Baptist Vision:

# The Bible

Other volumes in the series include:

# Proclaiming the Baptist Vision:

# The Bible

Walter B. Shurden
editor

Smyth & Helwys Publishing, Inc.
Macon, Georgia

ISBN 1-880837-98-6

*Proclaiming the Baptist Vision:*
*The Bible*

Walter B. Shurden, editor

Copyright © 1994
Smyth & Helwys Publishing, Inc.
Macon, Georgia

"Baptists, the Bible, and Authority" by Hugh Wamble is reprinted from *American Baptist Quarterly* with permission of The American Baptist Historical Society, Valley Forge, Pennsylvania 19482-0851.

The paper used in this publication meets the minimum requirements of American Standard for Information Sciences—Permanence of paper for Printed Library Materials, ANSI Z39.48–1984.

Library of Congress Cataloging-in-Publication Data

The Bible / Walter B. Shurden, editor.
    vi + 164  pp.                    6 x 9"  (15 x 23 cm.)
    ISBN 1-880837-98-6
    1. Bible--Criticism, interpretation, etc.  2. Bible--Sermons.
3. Sermons, American.  I. Shurden, Walter B.
BS511.2.B48  1994
220'.08'8261--dc20                                      94–7844
                                                        CIP

# Contents

### III. The Spiritual Formation of Our Lives and the Bible

### IV. Some Baptist Readings of the Bible

# Introduction

## *by Walter B. Shurden*

I first met the Holy in life when I was eighteen years old, a very green freshman at Delta State College in Cleveland, Mississippi. It was the spring of the year and new life was bursting all around me, a good and appropriate time, in the words of John's Gospel, to be "born again." I would later learn the spiritual life to be not a singular event with all the emphasis at the starting gate but a series of conversions, a saga of constantly being turned toward the Holy and of repeatedly, deliberately, and intentionally turning away. My journey, like most Christians I suppose, has been marred and scarred not primarily by what others have done to me or by the tragic in life but by the burden of my own humanity, by my own very serious and personal shortfall.

I understand completely what William Alexander Percy meant when he spoke of "stumbling through life by ear,"[1] but for me there has been a bit more than my own ear to guide. I would not have stumbled this far down the road without the incredible graces of life. Those graces are many: wife, children, parents, siblings, friends—lots of friends—local churches, and professors, to name a few. In addition to these more personal graces, one of God's graces to me has been the Bible.

The first Bible I ever owned was, of course, a King James version, and, of course for one of my generation (a youth in the 1950s) and location (the Mississippi Delta), a Scofield edition. In fact, my Bible was a brown leather Scofield edition of the King James. My name was on the cover in gold. To this very day I can remember the "smell" and the "feel" of that book. I kept it for years, marking it up with alternately red and black underlinings and with copious handwritten notes in the margins and at the top and bottom of the pages. Sermon notes, some of my own and some I had pirated while listening to other preachers, filled the blank pages at the front and at the back of that Bible.

I can remember wanting my Bible to look worn, read, studied, and used; I wanted people to believe that I loved that book. Indeed,

I would take it in my hands and "bend" it so that it would have a limp look, one that reflected lots of combat time. Beyond that eighteen-year-old bit of hypocrisy, however, and as honestly as I know how to say it, "I did love that book." I loved that particular edition and that particular size and color of the Bible. I loved to study it, to memorize it, to quote it. I loved it because I believed that it was in some mysterious way God's Holy Word to struggling humanity. I believed that at age eighteen, and I also believe that now with almost fifty-eight years of sand having dropped. While my way of looking at and understanding the Bible has changed significantly, my love for the Bible, rather than eroding, has deepened through the years.

Most of the contributors to this volume have had a romance with the Bible similar to that described above. To be sure, not all have had my particular journey with the Bible, but all of them, I dare say, would attest to the growing significance of the Bible in their lives. As you read their sermons it will be clear to you that they believe it, and that they believe it important to the Christian community in general and the Baptist community in particular.

It will also be clear that they do not believe the Bible to be a religious talisman, a kind of ecclesiastical rabbit's foot. Few, if any, of these writers would be comfortable with some of the more extreme conservative descriptions of the Bible—"inerrant," for example. Just as they would refuse to permit an extreme liberalism with its left-wing kind of rationalism to take the Bible away from them, so they would also refuse to allow an extreme fundamentalism with its right-wing rationalism to destroy the Bible for them.

This book is the second volume in a five-volume series entitled "Proclaiming the Baptist Vision." The idea of the series is simple: to present historic Baptist distinctives by way of sermons. The first volume, published in 1993 by Smyth & Helwys, was *Proclaiming the Baptist Vision: The Priesthood of All Believers*. This second volume focuses on the Baptist emphasis of the authority of scripture. Future volumes will include one each on the church, religious liberty, and the ordinances of baptism and the Lord's supper.

As I tried to indicate in the introduction to the first volume, I have no intention in this series of sermons on Baptist distinctives of suggesting that Baptists are the only ones God has or even the best that God has. Nor do the contributors to these volumes want to suggest such. The Baptist tradition, as every other expression of the Body of Christ, is founded upon the biblical affirmation that Jesus Christ is Lord. Baptists, as several of the sermons in this volume will argue, are a profoundly Christocentric people. In this regard, however, we are only acknowledging the cornerstone conviction of the church universal. The contributors to these volumes are Baptists, but they are Baptists who recognize that Baptists of the world represent only one distinctive branch of the magnificent Christian tree.

Even those principles that are usually identified as "Baptist distinctives" are not exclusively Baptist. The lists of these distinctives are many and somewhat varied. Usually, however, such a list would include the authority of the Bible, believers' baptism, a non-sacramental view of the Lord's Supper, religious liberty and voluntarism in matters spiritual, the priesthood of all believers, and local church independence, to name a few. Many Christian denominations would pay allegiance to one, several, or all of these so-called Baptist distinctives, so, Baptists can make no exclusive claim even to those principles that help define their denominational identity.

Baptists can certainly make no unique claim to biblical authority. I have for the last twenty-five years taught a class in three different colleges and seminaries entitled "Religious Groups in America." Representatives of the various faith groups come to class to "introduce" their particular Christian denomination or faith group to the students. Invariably and consistently, each of the representatives of the Christian denominations—Catholic, Orthodox, Episcopal, Lutheran, Presbyterian, Disciples, Assembly of God, Church of Christ, Pentecostal, and many others—begin with some version of the following sentence: "The authority for our church is the Bible." Christian sincerity demands that we take them at their word. Taking each other at our word on this issue means quite clearly that no single denomination is distinctive in claiming biblical authority for life and faith.

I hope that the fifteen sermons in this volume will assist both the Baptist laity and clergy in understanding better some of the approaches that Baptists take toward the Bible. Preachers often need some non-esoteric literature to place in the hands of their laity regarding issues in Baptist life. This book and other volumes in this series are designed to meet this need. Likewise, I would hope that this volume may help our non-Baptist friends understand that not all Baptists are fundamentalists who fear a non-fundamentalist approach to scripture and that non-fundamentalist Baptists certainly are not people who have lost their love for the Bible.

Of course, I hope that preachers, Baptists and otherwise, will also find some help in preaching about the Bible from these sermons. Like many who read these pages, I was sternly admonished during theological education by well-meaning seminary professors to avoid reading other preachers' sermons. I never believed that advice; I certainly have never followed it, nor have I met many preachers who did. My professors, I think, really wanted me to beware of becoming a pulpit parasite, of letting other people do my biblical exegesis, my theological reflection, and my contemporary application. Surely, this is a danger, but the danger runs in the other direction as well. The preacher can work so much in isolation that she or he comes to think there is only one way to mine the riches of the Bible or to theologize its implications for contemporary life. At any rate, these sermons are not designed to engender homilectical laziness but to act as a catalyst on the preacher's creativity.

In addition to this introduction and the concluding historical essay by the late Hugh Wamble, the body of this book consists of fifteen sermons by Baptist pastor-scholars and scholar-pastors. Almost all of the contributors have served as Baptist pastors at one time. Six are presently serving as pastors, six are serving in academic life among Baptists, and three are retired from full-time ministry. Each person has an abiding interest in the ministry of the pulpit, the art and science of preaching. Contributors were not asked to present a sermon with a certain slant on the Bible, only that they say, as a Baptist, what they most wanted to say.

The sermons, without intended design, fall into four general categories. The first four address in one way or another "The Theological Nature of the Bible." The second four sermons confront the inevitable and knotty issue of "The Task of Interpreting the Bible." The next four sermons, somewhat more practical in nature, focus on "The Spiritual Formation of our Lives and the Bible." While all of the sermons read and interpret the Bible through Baptist lenses, the last three sermons present more explictly "Some Baptist Readings of the Bible."

The lead sermon in this volume is by Ralph Elliott, a leading biblical scholar among Baptists, who, reared among Southern Baptists, spent much of his influential ministry, prior to retirement, as a pastor of American Baptist churches. Addressing the ancient question asked of Jeremiah, "Is there any word from the LORD?" Elliott answers unequivocally:

> Our Baptist heritage would not allow us to forsake the question nor would we desire to do so. Our birth as a people is rooted in the conviction that there is a word from the LORD and that somehow that word is connected with Holy Scripture.

Elliott calls Baptists to distinguish between the Bible as "a wooden past and a witnessing present." Aware of the early history of the Baptist people, Elliott says accurately that those Baptists were "an experiential people inspired by a living word, a word of witness, and leaving behind dead law and stale tradition."

Clyde Fant, internationally known expert on preaching, is a lifelong Baptist. In a most provocative and insightful sermon, Fant is concerned to demonstrate how Baptists can go about "Reaching Out With the Bible" in a cultural context for which the Bible is no longer "proof" or "authority." No Christian group can reach out to any culture, Fant suggests, without rightly understanding the essential nature of the Bible.

Wayne Stacy, Senior Minister of the First Baptist Church in Raleigh, North Carolina, is one of the creative voices among Baptists today and will be heard from even more in the future. Like Elliott and Fant, Stacy deals with the undergirding theological issue of divine revelation to human beings. He interprets, for example, the recent Southern Baptist controversy over the Bible as in fact a basic and fundamental argument over the nature of God. He gets at his vision of the Bible by answering two questions: Who is God, really? and How does God work in the world?

The final sermon focusing on the theological nature of the Bible comes from Glenn Hinson, one long known for his advocacy of authentic spirituality among Baptists. Hinson issues a prophetic call for Baptists to believe once again in "The Compelling Power of the Word of God." He argues that the contemporary church, Baptists included, for all our brags about the Bible, probably does not really believe the Bible has power apart from our clever handling of it.

The second group of sermons deals with what theologians call the hermeneutical question, how one goes about interpreting the Bible. Frank Stagg, Southern Baptists' premier New Testament scholar for the last third of the twentieth century, has been working at biblical interpretation for over six decades. Stagg highlights the importance at getting at the *intention* of the biblical text in order to rightly appropriate it. Says Stagg, "For Baptists historically, the Bible stands under no creed or council but is to be understood in terms of its own nature, content, and manner."

Paul Fiddes, principal of Regent's Park College at Oxford University in England, calls for a commitment to "The Demand beyond the Commands." His sermon is not simply a summons for serious biblical interpretation, it is a case study of such from John 5. To some extent like Frank Stagg, Fiddes wants to show the intent of scripture, but he does so by arguing that the ultimate intention of all of scripture is obedience to the will of God. What really mattered for Jesus, says Fiddes, was "God's will and purpose, and all moral and religious rules had to take second place to this. The commands given through Moses and the prophets were sign-posts, not chains; they were principles but not prisons."

Hardy Clemons, pastor of one of the flagship Baptist churches in the South, the First Baptist Church of Greenville, South Carolina, affirms the truthfulness of the Bible, but goes on to acknowledge that it contains different kinds of truth. Discerning the type of truth one is confronting when reading the Bible is basic to good biblical interpretation, says Clemons.

In her beautiful and challenging sermon, Elizabeth Barnes, professor of theology and ethics at Baptist Theological Seminary at Richmond, demonstrates how the stories of the Bible interlace our stories. Biblical interpretation comes by way of careful identification. Barnes reminds us that the living story of the Bible continues through the Christian community, and she calls Baptists to be a part of that continuing saga. Therein Baptists learn that things do not have to be like they are; we can change them.

The third group of sermons, certainly not unaware of the theological nature of the Bible or the arduous responsiblilty of biblical interpretation, identifies one of the major emphases of biblical authority for Baptists—its place in the life of the individual Christian. Charles Poole, pastor of the First Baptist Church in Macon, Georgia, entitles his sermon "Caution!" because he believes that "if we hear the Bible honestly and take the Bible seriously, we will be changed." He recognizes, however, that the Bible can be used in certain ways so as to avoid the pain of change.

Fisher Humphreys, a theology professor at Beeson Divinity School, takes the opportunity in his sermon to answer two questions about the Bible: "How does the Bible form our lives?" and "How can we use the Bible in such a way as to open our lives to its formative power?" The Bible, says Humphreys, is composed of literature that is "window-writing" and "mirror-writing."

> Window-writing is writing that we look through, to see beyond ourselves and our world to something transcendent. Mirror-writing is writing that we look into, to see a reflection of ourselves and our world so that we can understand them better.

Robert B. Setzer, Jr., like Wayne Stacy, Charles Poole, and Karen Smith, is someone Baptists will increasingly look to for future leadership. Fully aware of the need for critical study of Holy Scripture, Setzer is concerned that some Baptists get choked on the bones of critical Bible study rather than going for the meat of the matter. For Setzer, like other writers in this volume, the uniqueness of the Bible—the meat of the matter—is the One to whom it points. Bob Setzer is also concerned to show that the Bible should be studied within the context of the larger Christian community, including its scholars on whose shoulders we all stand and its faithful laity who live out its precepts.

A Baptist church historian who serves in a dual role as lecturer at South Wales College in Cardiff and minister of the Orchard Place Baptist Church in Neath, Wales, Karen Smith surely speaks for all Baptists when she calls the Bible "The Best Book of All." Drawing upon her knowledge of both Baptist history and the Bible, she illustrates how the Bible formed the lives of our denominational ancestors and how it can do the same for us. Like other preachers in this volume, she wants the written word to become the Living Word within us.

The final section of sermons is more specifically related to a Baptist reading of the Bible. William E. Hull, provost, Samford University, is a former pastor and New Testament professor. Drawing on both of these rich experiences of theological scholarship and ministerial practice, Hull identifies "How Baptists Read the New Testament." They read it, he contends, or at least they should, in light of three marks of the apostolic community: the centrality of Christ, the leadership of God's Spirit, and the mission of the church.

Steve Shoemaker, talented pastor of Broadway Baptist Church in Ft. Worth, Texas, follows the lead of theologian James McClendon and spells baptist with a small b. In his sermon he tells why, while also enumerating "the marks of the baptist way of being Christian and reading scripture." Flowing from this vision of being baptist, according to Shoemaker, is a somewhat distinct baptist way of preaching that he describes.

George Beasley-Murray, having taught in England, other parts of Europe, and the United States, is one of the best known names in the Baptist world today. Confessing that "Baptists are not distinguished from other Christians by a special view of the Bible that no one else in all the world holds" or "marked off from other churches by preaching a gospel that no one else believes," Beasley-Murray nonetheless presents the kind of gospel that Baptists preach as a result of how they read the Bible. Echoing a refrain that runs throughout the sermons in this book, he points to a Christocentric gospel.

The sermons in this book do not constitute *THE* Baptist vision of the Bible. Such does not exist. Indeed, one would find differences between the individual authors of these sermons. In the midst of these differences, however, is the conviction that the Bible is basic to the life of believers and Baptist churches.

Each volume in this series is to include one essay giving the reader a historical overview of how Baptists have dealt with the subject at hand since their beginning in seventeenth-century England. In the first volume my article entitled "The Priesthood of All Believers and Pastoral Authority in Baptist Thought" provided the historical context for understanding that issue among Baptists. For this volume on the Bible, I am using Hugh Wamble's excellent article published in the July, 1963, issue of *Foundations*. Wamble, long-time professor of Church History at the Midwestern Baptist Theological Seminary in Kansas City, Missouri, entitled the article "Baptists, The Bible, and Authority." Wamble's important article is reprinted here without alteration by permission of the American Baptist Historical Society.

I need to underscore a few facts about Hugh Wamble's essay. One, keep in mind as you read it that it was printed in July, 1963. The context for that article was the adoption by the Southern Baptist Convention of the revised "Statement of the Baptist Faith and Message" in Kansas City in 1963. Two, since the publication of that article over thirty years ago, the Southern Baptist Convention has undergone a radical change toward a dogmatic fundamentalism that only heightens the importance of Wamble's historical research, especially the significance of his conclusions. Wamble was one of those Baptist historians who always did very careful historical research in order to speak prophetically to contemporary needs. Three, while Wamble's article focused on a particular development in Southern Baptist life, his research (especially his closing section entitled "Threats to Scripture and Liberty of Conscience") is painfully relevant to all Baptists in all places at all times.

## Note

[1]William Alexander Percy, *Lanterns on the Levee* (Baton Rouge: Louisiana State University Press, 1941) 127.

# The Word as Witness

## *Ralph Elliott*

Thus says the Lord of hosts: Do not listen to the words of the prophets who prophesy to you; they are deluding you. They speak visions of their own minds, not from the mouth of the Lord. They keep saying to those who despise the word of the Lord, "It shall be well with you"; and to all who stubbornly follow their own stubborn hearts, they say, "No calamity shall come upon you."

> For who has stood in the council
> of the Lord
> so as to see and to hear his
> word?
> Who has given heed to his word
> so as to proclaim it?
> Look, the storm of the Lord!
> Wrath has gone forth,
> a whirling tempest;
> it will burst upon the head of
> the wicked.
> The anger of the Lord will not
> turn back
> until he has executed and
> accomplished
> the intents of his mind.
> In the latter days you will
> understand it clearly. (Jer 23:16-20)

Then King Zedekiah sent for him, and received him. The king questioned him secretly in his house, and said, "Is there any word from the Lord?" Jeremiah said, "There is!" Then he said, "You shall be handed over to the king of Babylon." (Jer 37:17)

# Introduction

In the midst of the ambiguities of life when it appears that individually there are no moral certainties and historically no dependable guides, "Is there any word from the LORD?"

This was the question continuously asked during Jeremiah's time. But unfortunately, like Zedekiah the last king of Judah, all generally wait until they are desperate before the question is asked with genuine seriousness. When the question is asked in desperation, the questioner is looking for a word personally favorable to the desperate situation. Rumbling Babylonian horse hoofs bearing down upon Judah were heard before King Zedekiah seriously asked the question. A storm had swirled through the palace when the king twice removed from Zedekiah, Jehoiakim, received a word that he did not wish to hear (Jer 36).

Even when the question is asked, whatever the motivation, a cacophony of sounds makes the proclamation dubious and the proclaimer competitive with a variety of voices.

This is the struggle the prophet Jeremiah faced. During a time of confused nationalism when Judah did double takes between Egypt and Babylon as to where security may lie, the prophet had been in lifelong conflict with others who had given messages diametrically opposed to his. In response to the question, "Is there any word from the LORD," both Jeremiah and his antagonists answered, "Yes," but their messages did not match. What does one do when many speak in the name of the same God, claiming authority, but with different messages?

Is this not where we are? Voices from the tele-airways sound one note and the community church on the corner sounds another. Brothers and sisters within the same denominational community violently disagree, and all claim positive affirmation in response to the question, "Is there any word from the LORD?"

Our Baptist heritage would not allow us to forsake the question, nor would we desire to do so. Our birth as a people is rooted in the conviction that there is a word from the LORD and that somehow that word is connected with Holy Scripture. The convictional gene of a biblically-based people constitutes the stuff of life. We are who we are because of an affirmative answer to King Zedekiah's question. Across the pages of history in every part of the globe, we have answered "there is" a word from the LORD, but obviously there is presently something defective about the transmission of the gene.

Jeremiah's people preceded us in the debate. His people believed that the word in their time was somehow related to the holy Torah, even as we know that it likewise is related to the sacred story. Can we learn from the earlier dispute? The question and answer asked elsewhere appear simple enough:

> Am I a God nearby, says the LORD, and not a God far off? Who can hide in secret places so that I cannot see them, says the LORD. Do I not fill heaven and earth? says the LORD (Jer 23:23-24).

God is near and there is a word through the Mosaic Torah, but the possession of the Torah must not lead to the mistaken assumption that God is simply a near God, easily and always at the beckoning call of the people—one whom they could summons by chapter and verse, manipulate by "thus sayeth the LORD" self-induced dreams and visions, or finalize by question and answer.[1] The prophet spoke of the nearness of God in a derogatory sense. The nearness of God cannot be absolutized by the mere transmission of a word from the past as if analogous to a textbook in law. Neither God's word nor the Presence can be absolutized as final. One can only give testimony to the Presence, near or far. By testimony to the Presence, the true word may be heard. There *is* always a word from the LORD, but it is a living word experienced through God's Presence rather than a coded word concretized in the past. The written word is no guarantee of the near-Presence of God.

## The Word as Witness

The contrast between a wooden past and a witnessing present touched me deeply in a recent visit. It was my privilege to spend a week in the little home where my father lived for many years prior to his death in 1985. The house was to be vacated as my stepmother made preparation to move into a retirement facility. One of the tasks was to empty an old-fashioned trunk that had been placed in the basement by an aunt years prior to her recent death. The articles were all there just as she had placed them—paper bags, scraps of material remaining from quilting, a newspaper or two, some worn-out print dresses, lace long ago rotted and in shreds, and pieces of clothing banished by style. The musty smell was overwhelming, but it was a sentient reminder of a life lived by "thou shalts" and "thou shalt nots."

The goods and the process were reminiscent artifacts of an unhappy life—debris from yesterday that failed to be the bearer of any great positive emotion. Nothing we found brought any experience of vibrant life. On the other hand, one did not need to look in a trunk in quest of my father's legacy. His spirit filled the place. He was a simple man but with great values, loyalties, and wisdom far beyond what his limited fifth-grade education might suggest. Upon reflection I realize that what has stayed with me were not those few times when he "laid down the law," as certainly he did, but the wonderful witness of love, loyalty, and care that he lived out in our midst. The style was always the same whether it was when as a widower with four children under six years we lived with grandparents and aunt in an extended family, or whether it was the many years in a new marriage.

Was there any "word from the LORD" in that setting? Yes, perennially, but it was a word of witness guided by a gentle spirit, not a word of law.

## The Living Word

In those early days when our denominational ancestors moved from the chairs of Puritans to Separatists to Baptists, we were an experiential people inspired by a living word, a word of witness, and leaving behind dead law and stale tradition. When a prestigious group of ecumenical scholars, Moslem and Christian, jointly published a volume setting forth understandings of the word of God, the significant difference was that Islamic scholars viewed the Quran as a literal tradition, while the Bible was viewed as an interpretative tradition.[2] The static words of the Quran are law to be literally applied as *litera scriptura* based upon some "deposit" model of revelation. The biblical word is a "living word" behind and beyond the written word. The Lutheran preacher Paul Scherer somewhere spoke of the Bible as the "Word searching for words."

Jeremiah debated with the false prophets because they thought their possession of the concrete Mosaic Torah was equal to the indestructible word. Jeremiah understood *that* word as a word of witness, a word of witness to a Presence and a voice larger than the preserved tradition.

Jesus constantly challenged his native community to correct the mistakes of the legalistic past in the recognition that Torah is not "law" in the legal sense, but witness, teaching, principle, and instruction, and that beyond the written book of law are mysteries beyond comprehension, ever subject to growing and accumulative interpretation. Thus we look upon the Bible not as a collection of texts proving some theory but as the living witness and promise of the Presence of God in the midst of a people.[3] This combination of divine-human words is not just historical information about something but a "dialogue of lovers"[4] where the story sometimes differs with itself, but where even discrepancies and disharmonies in the story carry the witness of a loving, forgiving, judging, redeeming, and parenting God—ever Present and caring.

The living Word behind the words approaches when those words are shared in telling the story. Our forebears understood that. Flooding warm memories bathe the heartstrings as I remember the countless people who stood in simple services of prayer and devotion and told their story. We called them "testimonies," or "giving a witness." There was new strength in telling the old story, for to retell was to re-experience the fresh Presence needed for a new day.

Echoes come from Jeremiah in another place:

> Stand at the crossroads, and look,
>     and ask for the ancient paths,
>   where the good way lies; and walk
>     in it,
>   and find rest for your souls.(6:16)

This is no call to the stern orthodoxies and mechanics of an outworn day. Jeremiah denied *that* kind of call when he dealt with the false prophets. It is a realization, however, that if we are not part of a story with deep spiritual roots, part of a story that transcends our limited history, we are in serious trouble. People hear very little if some word is picked up from the past and deposited as a straightjacket. We may possibly hear much when the word shared is a witness to the larger story of grace of which the concrete word is only a small part. If we listen we come into the very Presence of the One who initiated the experience that gave birth to the story. What a thrilling experience to discover the scripture story as a "witness to the meaning of the historical events" rather than something "handed down as an immutable expression of divine order."[5]

## *The Listening Ear*

This word of witness, the experiential and living word, however, comes only as we develop the listening ear. We may intellectually know that the Gospels are a witness and not a biography,[6] but the words fall flat without the sensitivity to listen for those silences between the spoken sounds.[7]

Dietrich Bonhoeffer, the German Christian martyr, speaks of a twofold approach to scripture in developing the listening ear—the *objectifying* of scripture and the *subjectifying* of scripture. The *objectifying* approach involves the best possible use of available interpretative tools in an effort to ascertain the best text, the nature of the literature, and the historical setting—the who, why, when, where, and how of the word. This is only preparation, however, and ultimately one must move from such an *outsider* stance to the *subjectifying, insider* stance.

As the Spirit is awaited, one listens for the treasure of God's promise, not "in my understanding but in my heart."[8] The preparatory role has led to the ultimate role. The observations of judgment and reason come together with the commitment of faith. The ascertained text and context, breathed upon by the patiently waited-for Holy Spirit, cause that witnessing text to become a vehicle of revelation. An ancient event and interpreter have produced a witnessing record. As the Holy Spirit breathes and moves across the pages of the story and into the listening ear, a new spiritual event and fresh revelation leading to confessions of awe and joy. The Word of God that preceded scripture becomes the Word of God beyond scripture. Something is set in motion within our very being. What grace-blessed listening when we no longer address the text, the word of witness, but the word of witness addresses us! Through the listening ear, it is not a matter of applying a text, for texts are so easily mistakenly applied, as Jeremiah's dispute with the false prophets indicates. The text is not what is authoritative for my life; it is the Word, the experience that is given birth through the witness of the text.

## The Nature of the Word as Witness

What is the nature of the word as witness? At times we do not understand what we have. Such was true with the Constitution of the

United States in the early days of the country. It took an Abraham Lincoln to demonstrate that the Constitution is more than a hard and fast, cold, legal document but a word of witness whose contribution would grow across the ages. Lincoln's Gettysburg Address was actually a "new act of founding," when the spirit of equality for all, Black and White, suddenly dawned. Garry Wills wrote of Lincoln at Gettysburg:

> Lincoln is here not only to sweeten the air of Gettysburg, but to clear the infected atmosphere of American history itself, tainted with official sins and inherited guilt. He would cleanse the Constitution—not, as William Lloyd Garrison had, by burning an instrument that countenanced slavery. He altered the document from within, *by appeal from its letter to the spirit* . . . The crowd departed with a new thing in its ideological baggage.[9]

Jesus approached the scripture that way—in its spirit: "You have heard that it was said to those of ancient times. . . . But I say to you . . ." (Matt 5:21-22). Paul likewise understood that it is the spirit to that witness must be given: "for the letter kills, but the Spirit gives life" (2 Cor 3:6). Jeremiah struggled with false prophets who knew the letter but did not understand its spirit as a word of witness.

## The Word of Presence

That word of witness is always a word of Presence.

I noticed during my pastoral years that in crises times people were not helped if I took them a chapter-and-verse answer or some brilliant intellectual analysis of their predicament. Even when they asked, "Why?" they were looking for a spirit and not a letter, for a Presence and not an answer.

Jeremiah tried to arrest the evil course of a nation, only to be trampled down and thrown underfoot. His life was a record of cross bearing and national failure, but the word of witness bore him a sustaining Presence: "i am with you, I Am With You, I AM WITH YOU" (Jer 1:8). The one word of witness in biblical promise more than any other is that of Presence.

This is the invitation, an invitation to *experience* the Presence. The Genesis narratives stressed a dependable Providence watching over Joseph: "The LORD was with him . . . The LORD was with Joseph . . ." (Gen 39:2, 3, 21, 23). The invitation from Exodus and following, however, is a call to encounter a Presence; it is like the difference between a *doctrine* and an *experience*, a difference between the propositional and the experiential! This centerpiece of biblical witness is the primary note of John's gospel: "And the Word became flesh and lived (tabernacled) among us . . ." (John 1:14). In Genesis, that Presence in all of the created order was indicated by the Spirit of God hovering and weaving within creation itself (Gen 1), but the word of witness is about a personalized Presence! Moses lived by it: "I will be with you . . ." (Exod 3:12). The same Presence who breathed on the ancients (Gen 2) walks alongside in life, present in life itself as our advocate, counselor, guide, and comforter (John 14-16) and breathing on us again with the power of life (John 20:22).

This is the spirit in which Baptists have turned to the Bible, not as an answer book, but as testimony to a Presence, a Presence who blesses the witness and lives again in spiritual encounter.

## *The Duality of the Word of Witness*

Let us not, however, mistake the duality of that word of witness. We can count on the Presence. We have been certain of that as early named by the prophet: "Immanuel" (Isa 7:14), "God with us." But *how* is God with us? The false prophets struggled to declare that the Presence always means automatic blessing. Jeremiah knew that Presence also means judgment. Jesus demonstrated within his person the duality of that word of witness, both blessing and judgment.

In the United States we have so often assumed that we are some kind of "new chosen people" whom God is obligated to bless. What a tragedy to be so blinded by either patriotism or nationalism that, like certain priests and prophets, we cling "to tradition, to dogma, to things that had been true and vital for generations but were no longer so for this one, which turned exhausted truths into fetishes."[10] William Hudnut, former mayor of Indianapolis, preached a sermon in the Nixon White House in which he reminded us that "there is a great difference between worshiping God and domesticating him . . . between affirming 'My country for God' and boasting 'God for My country.' "[11] The present God is at times the beyond, smashing rocks into pieces (Jer 23:29). We cannot "horse-trade" but rather must see the duality of the word as either blessing or cursing, understanding that "God's immanence must always be seen in the context of his transcendence."[12]

It is this duality of the witness, however, which gives us such great hope. Promises of either blessing or judgment are always conditional. Some persons are disturbed that close scrutiny indicates that biblical words did not always come into reality, but this God to whom the word bears witness is a patient and compassionate God whose word is in process. Up to the very last, God sounds the call to repentance as the God of the second chance, the God of another chance.[13]

# Conclusion

"Is there any word from the LORD?"

In the human arrogance of youth, I gave an intellectual answer to that question and assumed that I possessed the sure word. Years later, in the humility of the deeper realms of the spirit, I discovered that the mere statement of proposition and affirmation, dogma and articulation may be no word at all. It is a happy privilege to reach beyond intellectual belief to faith and to discover that the word is always relational, that spiritual things are matters of the spirit rather than law, and that it is not necessary to have an intellectual answer to everything in order to have an answering Presence.

The point is that across the pages of the written witness, God has come to us in the unconditional, indestructible Word of Jesus Christ, the explosive Word on a cross that no one has been able to hide from view.

That is the Word behind all words. That is the Word in search of response. Jesus, God's living Word, is testimony to the word of witness.

Is there any word from the LORD? There always *is*.

## Notes

[1]Werner E. Lemke, "The Near and the Distant God: A Study of Jer 23:23-24 in its Biblical Theological Context," *Journal of Biblical Literature* 100 (April, 1981): 554.

[2]Muslim Christian Research Group, *The Challenge of the Scripture: The Bible and the Quran* (Maryknoll: Orbis Books, 1989) 6ff.

[3]Markus Barth, *Conversation with the Bible* (New York: Holt, Rinehart, and Winston, 1964) 308.

[4]Barth, 10.

[5]Paul D. Hanson, "Biblical Interpretation: Meeting Places of Jews and Christians," *Canon, Theology, and Old Testament Interpretation*, ed. Gene M. Tucker *et al.* (Philadelphia: Fortress Press, 1988) 34.

[6]Paul J. Achtemeier, *An Introduction to the New Hermeneutic* (Philadelphia: Westminster, 1969) 153.

[7]David Petersen, "Israel and Monotheism: The Unfinished Agenda," *Canon, Theology, and Old Testament Interpretation*, 181.

[8]Dietrich Bonhoeffer, *Meditating on the Word*, ed. and trans. David McI. Gracie (Nashville: Cowley Publications, 1986) 9.

[9]Garry Wills, *Lincoln at Gettysburg: The Words That Remade America* (New York: Simon and Schuster, 1992) 38-39. The underlining is mine.

[10]George Adam Smith, *Jeremiah* (New York: George H. Doran Company, 1923) 263.

[11]William H. Hudnut, III, *Minister Mayor* (Philadelphia: Westminster Press, 1987) 10.

[12]Lemke, 555.

[13]Smith, 263-64.

# Reaching Out with the Bible

## Clyde E. Fant

At first glance, what could be more agreed upon among Baptists than the importance of using the Bible in proclamation and witness? Did not the Protestant Reformation replace the mass with the Word? Is the Word not also a central part of our tradition as Baptists? Do not Baptist speakers invariably refer to us as "people of the Book"— without even the necessity of explaining which book?

The question is not as simple as it seems, however. Whatever degree of uniform opinion may once have existed is now gone.

Some persons feel that the Bible is often more hindrance than help in witness and even in preaching. They argue that contemporary persons could scarcely care less what the Bible says about anything, even if they should care. They believe that the Bible means nothing to most people today, that it is not authority to them, and that quoting it as authority only provokes ridicule or hostility, or at best, an indifferent shrug. Others argue that the Bible must be quoted extensively in both witness and preaching. They believe in beginning with a text and exegeting it verse-by-verse throughout the sermon, and they insist that anything less is not biblical preaching.

The entire question has become a battleground. Emotions scarcely can be aroused more by any other issue among us. If you do not believe this, notice how many times convention speakers have used the subject to evoke from the galleries thunderous "amens" loud enough to make the angels molt. Or, on the other hand, listen to the biting sarcasm of those who disagree.

Why this tension? How could people of a lengthy evangelical position come to such sharp disagreement?

Some pastors and laypersons reduce the entire matter to a one-word answer: heresy. Those who do not believe in the frequent quoting of the Bible in preaching and witness are weak in their belief in the Bible itself. They are embarrassed by it, and, worse, they do not really adhere to the Christian faith, even though they mouth certain terms and pretend to be loyal Christians. Others have another simple, one-word answer: ignorance. Those who continue to quote the Bible as though everyone must fall down at the magic phrase "the Bible says"—when the Bible has long since ceased to be authority for many people—are merely ignorant of the changing world.

But is the question that simple? Do invectives like "heretic" and "ignoramus" really explain the divergent viewpoints among us concerning the use of the Bible? In order to gain some understanding of the problem and at the same time find useful suggestions for a Baptist philosophy of reaching out with the Bible, we must look at the changing setting for Baptist work.

Until very recently, the uniformity of Baptist thinking on the use of the Bible was matched by the uniformity of the culture around us. It is probably safe to say that Baptists in the South have come out of the most uniform religious climate of any group since the Catholic church in medieval Spain. For most of our history, "the Bible says" was tantamount to a papal encyclical. Not that everyone in the South was Baptist—or a Christian of any sort—but such religion as there was, such religion as the average person encountered, was strongly evangelical and Bible-centered. Even to those who did not "take to religion," the Bible was still "the Good Book" and, like as not, when challenged by a passage from it they would feel embarrassment or guilt. Contrast that atmosphere with that of a contemporary college campus or corporate board room, even in the South, and you will understand a part of the problem.

Yet the problem is larger still. Baptists are a nationwide, and even worldwide, religious body. We are going toward the pluralism of the world while the world is moving in on us. More than ever before, diverse viewpoints are encountered in our preaching and witness. Fewer of our non-Christian neighbors come from our once uniformly Bible-respecting background. They are as surprised as we are by the differences people have in values. Communities in the South that have worked ceaselessly to "attract industry" are often resentful of the divergent viewpoints that such expansion brings.

On the other hand, the South still contains enormous pockets virtually untouched by these changing forces. Pastors and lay leaders in those areas vehemently argue that the Bible is still the same authority it ever was—because it is. They insist that the same approach works—because it does. Nevertheless, with the mass media today rapidly bringing divergent ideas into the most isolated areas, the days are numbered for these few areas that still enjoy this sociological lag.

It would be more comfortable, no doubt, to witness and preach in the old climate where everyone respected the Bible and would usually give the preacher a fair crack at them—if only once a year in a brush arbor meeting. But that is not our world; it is not coming back. Yet we must be honest with ourselves. Have we not traded on that climate to some extent? When it was easier to get a person to listen to sermons, was it not also easy to depend on social pressure to put him or her into the church? Are not many of our defections and drop-outs—and we have millions of them—not due to their leaving the uniform Baptist climate for other places where social pressure is in the other direction and where, having had no real conversion to the life in Christ, they soon drop their nominal, sociological religion?

Mark it well: Wherever and whenever in Christian history any group has enjoyed the numerical superiority and cultural uniformity that Southern Baptists had over the past century, a "national religion" develops, with all of its attendant problems of superficial agreement and latent hostility.

In the past, some young ministers were urged to leave the "gospel-hardened" areas to seek more fallow fields of work. I never liked that term. I realize that it means that individuals have become hardened *to* the gospel, rather than hardened *by* it. Nevertheless, I do not feel that it is an accurate term. People in the South did not become hardened to the Bible, but to the authoritarian and sometimes even belligerent use of it. This is not a problem confined solely to the South, either, as some who have gone into "pioneer" areas have discovered to their dismay. The South may be in the "Bible belt," but to some extent our nation is a "Bible belt." That is, while other areas besides the South do not as readily accept the Bible as authority, they know it is regarded as authority by many and may be equally defensive in the presence of it. In short, non-Christian Southerners know that the Bible is authority in their region, but they may resent being pressured by an authority to which they have never agreed themselves. Non-Christians in other areas may be even more emphatic in their resentment, because the Bible is neither the standard for their group nor have they accepted it.

What does this suggest for our situation today in the use of the Bible? Has the misuse of it as an authoritarian club caused it to become a negative symbol rather than a positive one? Has the Scripture-spouting hypocrite ruined the credibility of the Bible? Has the pulpit-pounding, Bible-curling, chair-smashing evangelist caused the Bible to become more of a liability than an asset in the proclamation of the gospel? What place should the Bible have in Baptist preaching and outreach?

First, we must understand that the spiritual truths of the Bible are not true because they are in the Bible, but because they are true. This suggests that while the Bible may be granted authority, it also contains authority. That is, loyal Christians may agree to a previously unknown dictum in the Bible because it is in the Bible, but we must remember that we only do so because our experience with the Word of God has so convinced us of its truth that we tend to grant it further authority. To expect non-Christians to agree on the same basis is obviously unfair. If we attack those who think otherwise, we cause them to reject the Word of God for the same reason we accept it: simply because the Bible says so.

In other words, to use the Bible as authority to prove its own content is to reason in a circle. It can only be used as such if there is a prior supposition: that non-Christians *already accept the Bible as authority*, even if they know little of it and live by even less of it. There is the problem. In the past we encountered many such individuals in Southern culture, and in some areas there are still many of them; but increasingly we are all forced to give witness to the Word before people to whom the Bible is not authority, and even may be negative authority.

Remember, however, that the faith of a Christian is anchored in the proposition that "God was in Christ"; that Jesus Christ is "the way, the truth, and the life"; and that when people know that truth, it shall make them free. In the past, many Baptists have been too preoccupied with finding a way to prove the gospel rather than a way to proclaim it. We may easily convince a person who has had "proof." If they begin by agreeing that the Bible is authority, then all we have to do is quote the appropriate passage, and *presto-change-o*, they are convinced and "converted."

But does the gospel really work that way? Can we eliminate the difficult step of faith? "So faith comes from what is heard, and what is heard comes through the word of Christ" (Rom 10:17). We are saved by grace through *faith*. Is it a commitment in faith that has been lacking in the sociological Christian. They believe in the gospel because the Bible says so, because the ethnic religion around them says so. When the string unwinds in the other direction—their new world no longer says so, and therefore the Bible doesn't have authority, so the gospel is wrong—then we are confronted with the typical name-on-the-roll-only problem child of the church.

We do not need to use the Bible less, but to use it less as author-ity. We must forsake the cheap conformities that pass for conversions. It is not proof that we need, but proclamation. "And without faith it is impossible to please God" (Heb 11:6). We must remember that the proper order in witness is the Word of God, hearing, and then faith. Each person must commit himself or herself to the Word. If we begin by trading on a cultural accommodation to the Bible as authority, we tend to begin with "proof" and wind up without faith.

But isn't this a risky business? Doesn't it allow people to decide anything they want about the gospel? Precisely. Faith is a risky business. It would be much neater and far better proof if God should split the heavens every day at noon and shout, "Shape up!" But God only has children by faith. If God is willing to risk the kingdom on the proclamation of the gospel and the response of faith, then so should we.

This suggests a solution to the problem posed at the beginning. The Bible is indispensable to both preaching and witness, because it tells us the truth about God. It is the record of the acts of God—historical, unique, non-repeatable. In recording the revelation of God, the Bible is that revelation, for someone here and now. We use the Bible because it is revelation, because it tells us things we don't know and can't find out otherwise. To use it as authority is to put the cart before the horse. We use it to tell the truth. We use it to proclaim the Good News. The Word of God is truth, and truth bears its own authority, but everyone may accept or reject the truth. To accept it is to act in faith. We proclaim it that persons may have the opportunity to act in faith.

"But how shall they hear?" is still the great question. If the use of the Bible presents such psychological and sociological problems to modern people, and the Bible contains the Word of God, how indeed shall they hear?

We must make every effort to convey the meaning of the gospel with its internal proof rather than authority of the Bible as an external proof. We must seek to communicate the truth of the gospel with the same spirit of loving understanding that Jesus possessed. Like Jesus before the "rich young ruler," we must present the challenge of discipleship while "looking upon them and loving them"; and like Jesus, we may also watch with sorrow as "they go away sorrowful."

This suggests that in preaching we do not need to quit the traditional use of the Bible as the revelation of the love of God, but that our specific contemporary use of it may vary. We must seek preaching that is truly biblical—not preaching that uses a given number of verses at a given place in the sermon or preaching that is arranged and outlined according to a mechanical, neo-scholastic scheme—but preaching that delivers the Word God sent, preaching that is determined to be a servant of the Word. Biblical preaching cannot be equated with any external method. Even the devil can fill his mouth with scriptural quotations.

When the message of the gospel is allowed to address our real life, our true needs, then the Word reaches out to grasp us. Those who look for it are found by it. Then the ancient events become contemporary events in the experience of the hearers. For a child hearing the story, Zacchaeus climbs that tree for the first time; for the listening women, Christ gives living water to the woman at the well for the first time; for that man seeking a way of life, Christ today says, "Follow me."

When the gospel is proclaimed in such a way, whether in witness or in sermon, then we need not fear for proof nor hunger after authority, for the Word of God reaches out to seek and to save that which was lost.

# Risky Business

## R. Wayne Stacy

Now there was a Pharisee named Nicodemus, a leader of the Jews. He came to Jesus by night and said to him, "Rabbi, we know that you are a teacher who has come from God; for no one can do these signs that you do apart from the presence of God." Jesus answered him, "Very truly, I tell you, no one can see the kingdom of God without being born from above." Nicodemus said to him, "How can anyone be born after having grown old? Can one enter a second time into the mother's womb and be born?" Jesus answered, "Very truly, I tell you, no one can enter the kingdom of God without being born of water and spirit. What is born of the flesh is flesh, and what is born of the Spirit is spirit. Do not be astonished that I said to you, 'You must be born from above.' The wind blows where it chooses, and you hear the sound of it, but you do not know where it comes from or where it goes. So it is with everyone who is born of the Spirit." Nicodemus said to him, "How can these things be?" Jesus answered him, "Are you a teacher of Israel, and yet you do not understand these things?

"Very truly, I tell you, we speak of what we know and testify to what we have seen; yet you do not receive our testimony. If I have told you about earthly things and you do not believe, how can you believe if I tell you about heavenly things? No one has ascended into heaven except the one who descended from heaven, the Son of Man. And just as Moses lifted up the serpent in the wilderness, so must the Son of Man be lifted up, that whoever believes in him may have eternal life." (John 3:1-15)

## The Baptist Battle about God

Unless you've been hiding under a rock, you're almost certainly aware that from 1979 to 1990 Southern Baptists were embroiled in an angry debate that has had a devastating effect on almost every aspect of Baptist life. With embarrassing frequency, the media, both religious and secular, report on Baptist agencies succumbing to "hostile take-overs," seminaries being dismantled and de-funded, employees being summarily dismissed. It's a sorry spectacle that has touched us all over the past fifteen years. None of us who call ourselves "Baptist" is insulated from the painful effects of what has been charitably described as a "controversy."

What was it all about? To be sure, we Baptists are by nature a contentious lot, and therefore controversy is nothing new among us.[1] This recent debate became so bellicose, however, that it has unraveled the fragile fabric of fellowship and cooperation Southern Baptists have enjoyed for nearly 150 years. What was the fuss all about?

The answer depends upon whom you ask. On the one hand, some persons say that the issue was theological, pure and simple. They suggest that certain "liberals" (as they define the term) crept into the denomination—particularly in the seminaries, colleges, boards, and agencies—and threatened to subvert the Southern Baptist Convention from its conservative, Bible-believing traditions. Just what precisely constitutes "liberalism," however, is something of a mystery. Ask three Baptists to define what a liberal is and you'll most likely get at least four answers! One pastor of a large, urban church probably gave the most honest answer to the question when he told an interviewer: "A liberal is anyone who doesn't believe like I do."

Another interpretation, however, says that the problem had little or nothing to do with theology, but was rather concerned with "power politics," pure and simple. This point of view argues that *all* Southern Baptists are conservative theologically and that the charge of "liberalism" is a smoke screen to hide the real agenda—who controls the power in the nearly fifteen-million-member denomination. They cite as evidence the now well-documented account of how one of the architects of the fundamentalist strategy to take over the denomination actually rented "sky-boxes" at the annual meeting of the convention when it convened in the Astrodome in Houston in 1979, and from that vantage point orchestrated the work of his lieutenants on the floor below who then directed messengers, who had been bussed in for the purpose, how to vote, thus ensuring the election of their candidate for president of the Southern Baptist Convention.[2] Some of the so-called "moderates" say, therefore, that the real issue has been power—specifically, the desire of a few, highly-visible pastors to seize control of the entire denomination and to dictate how the denomination is run.

The question is, "Who is right?" Has the dilemma been a theological one or a political one? Actually, it's some of both. The dilemma is, I believe, both one of politics and theology.

While the political ramifications in terms of the attempt to control property, personnel, and resources are easy to see, the theological implications are far more oblique. While most of what you heard and read suggested that the controversy among Southern Baptists focused on what one has described as "The Battle for the Bible," the real battle is taking place on a more basic battleground—*what do you believe about God?*

Underneath all this rhetoric about the "nature of the Bible" are two fundamental questions: Who is God really? and How does God work in the world? It's not just a debate over the nature of scripture; it's a debate over the nature of God! That's why I say that at least a part of the problem is indeed theological, and I mean "theological" in the most basic sense of the term—the God-question. What do you really believe about God, and how do you think God works in the world? That, I think, is at the heart of the recent Baptist fight.

## Who Is God, Really?

If, as Baptists, the Bible is to be our guide—that is, if we don't just talk about the Bible, but actually read it—then the answer to the first question, Who is God really?, is clear: God is the only uncreated reality in the universe. The most basic affirmation of the Judeo-Christian tradition is the oneness of God. Israel's credo, the Shema, says it plainly: "Hear, O Israel, the LORD is our God and the LORD is one" (Deut 6:4, writer's translation). The most foundational affirmation of biblical faith is the oneness of God, not the singularity of God—as the Christian revelation of the Triune God makes clear— but the oneness of God.

This basic affirmation about God has profound and far-reaching implications. For example, C. S. Lewis said that the image of the oneness of God means, at bottom, that only two categories of reality really exist: uncreated reality—that which has Life in Itself and is utterly autonomous, dependent upon nothing for its continued existence—and created reality, wherein life is derivative and dependent.[3] The biblical revelation is that only God rightly belongs in the "uncreated" category and that *everything else* belongs in the "created" category.

That essential division between "created" and "uncreated" reality probably stands behind the Old Testament injunction regarding love of God and neighbor which figured so prominently in Jesus' theology: "You shall love the Lord your God with all your heart, and with all your soul, and with all your strength, and with all your mind; and your neighbor as yourself" (Luke 10:27). In other words, we are to love uncreated reality in one way—with total abandon and with the totality of ourselves—and created reality in another. Total devotion is totally reserved for the Creator alone. Words like "inerrant" and "infallible" are appropriate when the subject is God but nothing else, because there is a qualitative, insuperable distinction between "creature" and "Creator." That's biblical faith.

## How God Works in the World

Likewise, if we look to the biblical revelation for an answer to the second question—How does God work in the world?—the answer is equally clear: *incarnationally*. God, The Uncreated One, comes among His creatures so that God might make Himself known to them. That's always been God's way, taking flesh, taking life, walking down my street and calling me by name. In the act of creation, in God's special revelation to Israel, in sending His Son, and in entrusting to us His Word in the scriptures, God moves among us incarnationally, the Creator among the creatures.

That's risky business, because incarnation implies accessibility, and accessibility implies vulnerability. Indeed, accessibility and vulnerability always stand in a one-to-one relationship. You see, a thief can break into your home and steal your jewelry and your TV, but that's about all the thief can do to you. But your family can devastate you. Why? Because they have access to places the thief can never go. Accessibility and vulnerability always stand in a one-to-one relationship. The God of the Bible is a God who walks down my street and calls me by name!

The problem is, this incarnational way God works is diametrically opposed to the way we would like for God to do it—with guarantees and collateral. You see, there's risk in incarnational revelation, and we don't like risk.

In John's Gospel, where Jesus is the very revelation of God, the Word of God, the prologue says: "And the Word became flesh and dwelt among us, and *we* (italics mine) beheld its glory, glory as of the only begotten of the Father, full of grace and truth." Did you get that? Did you hear the shift in language? "The Word became flesh." Language of fact. "And we beheld its glory." Language of confession. The implication is clear: While some saw the Glory of God in that "flesh," others just saw flesh. Why wasn't it obvious so that everybody would understand? Because to be human is, by its very nature, to enter a world of subtlety and ambiguity and infinite possibility where nothing is fail-safe and guaranteed.

When I was a professor at one of our seminaries, I taught a course on the Synoptic Gospels. Part of the purpose of the course was to introduce the students to this whole business of multiple, but not identical, accounts of the same event and the implications this has for the nature of scripture. I determined that the best way to do that was to let the students discover this for themselves rather than my just talking about it. And so I gave them an exercise in which they were asked to read an account of the same event in each of the Synoptic Gospels, Matthew, Mark, and Luke, and then underline in different colors the words unique to each Gospel, the words common to all three, and the words common to just two. When they finished the exercise, both the similarities and the differences between the three accounts of the same event were obvious and irrefutable.

Some students, those whose view of scripture was monolithic and singular, all black and white with no ambiguity, just couldn't handle the differences they'd discovered. "Well, which one is right?" was all they wanted to know. They wanted it nailed down, fixed, without ambiguity, and the Gospels just weren't cooperating! What's more, some actually became angry with me for making them do the exercise in the first place. I was the messenger who had born the bad news about the good news. One student actually said to me: "I would rather have not known." I hope he never becomes your pastor!

We don't like that, do we? Ambiguity, loose ends. We want it all nailed down with contracts and study guides and Bibles that don't make you think. But it's a child's world where there's all light and no shadows. So some students—not all but some—come to the seminary for a degree instead of an "education," the presence of which no paper can adequately document nor the absence of which no degree can adequately remedy. That's the way we like things—predictable, fail-safe and risk-free. And that's the way we want our religion too. We want a God who's manageable, predictable, safe, who does things by the book—and I do mean *by the Book*—who walks the dog at the same time every morning and never colors outside the lines.

More than any other single theological factor, I think, *that* lies at the heart of the Baptist dilemma regarding the Bible. We don't like this *incarnational* way God does things. We want a faith that is predictable, manageable, fail-safe, and risk-free.

That's why some are not willing to take the Bible for what it is—God's Word mediated through human personality, God's Word in human words. "But if the Bible, like any other book, uses *human* words to convey *God's* Word, then, like any other attempt at communication, isn't it capable of misinterpretation and ambiguity and complexity? We can't have that." We prefer a God who backs us into a corner and says: "Alright now you weasel, believe!" We don't want faith; we want proof. Thus we seek to ease the tension that is life as God gives it by concretizing God in some palpable and manageable form. An "inerrant" Bible! That'll do it!

Now, to be sure, there are religions which do in fact espouse faith in a God who reveals himself in ways untouched by human hands, hermetically sealed off, as it were, from any human contamination. The original copy of the *Koran*, it is claimed, is kept in heaven, unspoiled and protected from human taint. The *Book of Mormon* was found, it is claimed, under a rock in New York State, having been placed there by an angel of God.

But the God of the Bible seems not to do things that way. God pays us, as C. S. Lewis says, "the intolerable compliment of loving us in the deepest, most tragic, most inexorable sense."[4] God gives us room to decide, to choose, to say "no" if we will to the very one without whom we would not, we could not, even be. God comes among us, accessible and vulnerable, whispering a Word of Grace, and we've got to risk it all on the belief that: "You know, I *think* I heard it! I *think* I saw it!"

Fred Craddock, retired professor of preaching at Emory University, tells a story about traveling in Israel and being taken by his Jewish guide to Shepherd's Field near Bethlehem to visit the place where Christ's birth was reportedly announced to the shepherds.[5] He says that his guide, in telling the story, pointed to the city of Bethlehem over on the hill nearby and explained to Craddock that sometimes on clear nights, the stars would shine so brightly on the horizon over Bethlehem that it would appear as if some of them were actually resting on top of the city.

"Perhaps that's what the wise men saw that night in Bethlehem," he said to Craddock.

Of course, the guide, was mixing Matthew and Luke. But Craddock, wishing to be deferential and yet not apologetic for his own faith said: "Well, that's certainly *one* explanation for what happened."

To which the Jewish guide said: "Oh, I know that's just *one* explanation. When I was in school, I had a rabbi who said that if something happened that couldn't be explained *another way*, you could be sure that God didn't do it!"

That's not bad. As a matter of fact, that's pretty good biblical theology.

John's Gospel gives us a story on this very theme. A man came to see Jesus one night, Nicodemus was his name. He came "at night" because he was a card-carrying member of the Sanhedrin, and he was supposed to be the one with the answers, not the questions. He was a buttoned-down, squared away kind of guy, but he thought he'd seen something in this rabbi that unsettled him and threatened to disrupt his orderly, pin-striped world. So he deftly approached his subject with enough finesse to make a career diplomat blush: "Rabbi, we know that you are a teacher come from God, for no one could do these signs you do, unless God be with him."

But Jesus would not be so easily schmoozed: "Nicodemus, enough of these amenities! Let's cut to the chase. You need to be born again."

Now, as do all John's stories, this story moves on two levels. Nicodemus *thought* Jesus was saying one thing when, in fact, Jesus was saying something else, and Nicodemus didn't get it. The point of the story turns on the double meaning of the word translated "again" in the Greek—*anothen*—which can mean either "again" or "from above." Get it? Jesus was saying: "Nicodemus, you must be born *from above*, that is, from *God*. You must embrace a totally different orientation to life!" But Nicodemus thought he meant merely that he must be born "again," as in twice!

"How can a man enter the second time into his mother's womb and be born? That's not logical!"

Jesus said: "You dolt!" (I'm paraphrasing.) "I didn't say you must be born *again*, I said you must be born *again*, as in *from above!*" And then, he went on to give Nicodemus, *and us* (the "you" is now plural) a lesson on how God does things.

"Nicodemus, it's like the wind. You can't see it, or capture it, or manage it or control it. It's not what you there in the Sanhedrin think it is: the logical conclusion to an argument. God is not some 'Subject' for debate! The kind of life God gives is like the wind; it blows where it wills, and you can feel the force of it. But don't try to manage it or manipulate it." John did it again, his "double speak," for the Greek word for "wind" is the same word as "Spirit."

"Life of the *Spirit*, Nicodemus, is gift, pure and simple! It's from above, out of the blue, unearned, unachieved, uncontrolled, uncalculated. It's as mysterious as the whence and whither of the *wind*! You don't manage it. God isn't a 'test question' you can either get right or wrong! You believe or you don't believe. Because, you see, if you believe, final proof isn't necessary. But if you don't, final proof is never quite enough."

"Don't be queasy, Nicodemus, when I say 'you must be born *from above!*' No proofs, no money-back guarantees, no inerrant Bibles to prop up a faith that can't handle ambiguity and loose ends. God won't drag you into the kingdom kicking and screaming."

"The Word has become flesh. Whether you see glory in that flesh, or just flesh, you must choose. And you must run the risk that what is so clear to you, others won't see at all!"

"But what you cannot have, Nicodemus, is a faith that *costs* you nothing, *risks* nothing, *asks* nothing, without struggle, without vulnerability, or decision. That's just not the way God does things."

Trusting a God like this is risky business!

There's an old Hasidic story that goes like this:[7] When Adam and Eve were expelled from Eden, they wasted no time blaming themselves. Instead, they blamed each other, thus establishing the pattern for married life through the ages. For a time they considered trying to sneak back into the Garden. But the gate looked forbidding and the angel with the flaming sword appeared incorruptible. So, with many a backward glance, they began their journey over the face of the earth, looking for a place to dwell.

Some lands were too hot, others too cold. This place was a desert, that one a swamp. A few that looked and felt just right proved to be shared by large carnivores whose urgent appetites threatened life and limb. The long days of searching dragged painfully into years.

At last, the man and woman came to a large fertile valley. Sweet grasses grew abundantly in it, and a clear, fresh stream ran sparkling through its middle. Gentle animals grazed quietly, and fish leaped shining into the sunlight. Far up in one of the valley walls was a clean, dry cave, with an apron that caught the first rays of the dawn. Here the man and woman settled down.

Things went well for them. Adam tilled the ground and hunted for game. Eve prepared the food, sewed clothing, and grew great with child. Oh, it wasn't Eden! The night the skunk got into the butter crock Eve wept and remembered the Garden. The day his plow broke on a large boulder Adam cursed and reminded his wife about the apple.

But then one night in spring, when the air was soft and fragrant with the scent of new growth, Adam lay on the apron of the cave, unable to sleep. The sky above him was splashed with stars, the muted lowing of the herds came faintly from the pastures below. Every muscle in his body ached from the labors of the day.

Suddenly, Adam turned to his wife.

"Eve, God was wrong! *This* is what we were meant for! To till the ground and raise our grain. To hunt and fish for meat, to work all day in the hot sun and feel the sweat drying on our bodies in the cool of the evening. To risk everything trying something and failing and trying it again and failing again. To keep on trying until it works. To struggle to understand things that fill us with fear. To feel hunger and thirst and pain—and hope! This is better than Eden, Eve. *This* is what we were meant for! God was wrong, Eve. God was wrong!"

And, so the story goes, somewhere so far away that the human mind cannot even imagine the distance and so near that the breath of Adam's speaking was hot against His hand, God heard the defiant words flung by the little man into the deep well of space, and when He heard them, God smiled.

## Notes

[1]See, for example, Walter B. Shurden's *Not a Silent People: Controversies That Have Shaped Southern Baptists* (Nashville: Broadman Press, 1972).

[2]Cf. Grady C. Cothen, *What Happened to the Southern Baptist Convention?* (Macon GA: Smyth & Helwys Publishing, 1993) 6-7.

[3]Lewis works this idea out in several places in his writings, but perhaps the clearest treatment is found in a chapter called "The Naturalist and the Supernaturalist," in *Miracles* (New York: Macmillan Publishing Co., 1947) 5-11. See also his *Problem of Pain* (New York: Macmillan Publishing Co., 1940) 37ff.

[4]*Problem of Pain*, 41.

[5]Craddock has told this story on numerous occasions. I heard him tell it during a lecture series he was giving at William Jewell College in Liberty, Missouri, back in the late 1980s.

# The Compelling Power of the Word of God

## E. Glenn Hinson

While Peter and John were speaking to the people, the priests, the captain of the temple, and the Sadducees came to them, much annoyed because they were teaching the people and proclaiming that in Jesus there is the resurrection of the dead. So they arrested them and put them in custody until the next day, for it was already evening. But many of those who heard the word believed; and they numbered about five thousand.

The next day their rulers, elders, and scribes assembled in Jerusalem, with Annas the high priest, Caiaphas, John, and Alexander, and all who were of the high-priestly family. When they had made the prisoners stand in their midst, they inquired, "By what power or by what name did you do this?" Then Peter, filled with the Holy Spirit, said to them, "Rulers of the people and elders, if we are questioned today because of a good deed done to someone who was sick and are asked how this man has been healed, let it be known to all of you, and to all the people of Israel, that this man is standing before you in good health by the name of Jesus Christ of Nazareth, whom you crucified, whom God raised from the dead. This Jesus is

'the stone that was rejected by
you, the builders;
it has become the cornerstone.'

There is salvation in no one else, for there is no other name under heaven given among mortals by which we must be saved."

Now when they saw the boldness of Peter and John and realized that they were uneducated and ordinary men, they were amazed and recognized them as companions of Jesus. When they saw the man who had been cured standing beside them, they had nothing to say in opposition. So they ordered them to leave the council while they discussed the matter with one another. They said, "What will we do with them? For it is obvious to all who live in Jerusalem that a notable sign has been done through them; we cannot deny it. But to keep it from spreading further among the people, let us warn them to speak no more to anyone in this name." So they called them and ordered them not to speak or teach at all in the name of Jesus. But Peter and John answered them,

"Whether it is right in God's sight to listen to you rather than to God, you must judge; for we cannot keep from speaking about what we have seen and heard." After threatening them again, they let them go, finding no way to punish them because of the people, for all of them praised God for what had happened. For the man on whom this sign of healing had been performed was more than forty years old. (Acts 4:1-22)

I've debated with myself whether hope for the 1990s lies in freedom for the Word of God or simply in the Word itself. On lengthy reflection I'm inclined to say that the Word itself is our hope.

When I speak about the Word of God, I'm not talking only about the Bible. The Bible is, as Luther put it, the cradle of the Word, but it can only be thought of as the Word of God in a qualified sense. The Word of God is God's self-disclosure, revelation itself, and pace inerrantists, not every word in the Bible is revelation itself. The Word cannot be confined to a book or human efforts to convey it.

In scriptures the Word of God is dynamic. God speaks, and the world comes into being. God speaks, and saving revelation occurs. God speaks, and the Word redeems. God's Word, so God says through Isaiah, "shall not return to me empty," (Isa 55:11). "Indeed, the word of God is living and active, sharper than any two-edged sword," according to the author of Hebrews (4:12), "piercing until it divides soul from spirit, joints from marrow; it is able to judge the thoughts and intentions of the heart."

A Word such as this does not need human agencies to effect freedom; it will do its work whether human beings give permission or not. It would be the height of human presumption to assume that mere mortals could control the Word of God. Human beings can respond to or reject, but they do not control the Word.

## The Compelling Character of the Word

The Word of God, revelation, has a compelling character. "We cannot keep from speaking about what we have seen and heard," the Apostles replied to the Sanhedrin's order to stop preaching and teaching everywhere in the name of Jesus. What they had seen and heard—about the life, death, and resurrection of Jesus—had taken hold and would not let them go, even if it cost them their lives. Many other people have acted out of the same conviction:

• The early Christian martyrs could have saved their lives had they only been willing to say, "Caesar is Lord!" and to deny that Jesus is Lord. Their contemporaries couldn't understand how simple people died like philosophers. Perpetua's father, a person of wealth and culture, couldn't comprehend why his daughter, about to be martyred, would not come to her senses. "If you don't care about yourself," he pleaded, "at least think of your unborn child." But the Word had taken hold of this young woman's life, and she could not not speak what she had seen and heard.

• Monks carried the message to the barbarians in central and northern Europe. They could easily have held fast to the amenities of civilization but chose instead to risk life and limb for the Word. Severinus, the Apostle to the Danube, worked relentlessly among the fierce Germanic tribes north of the Danube and Rhine in modern Hungary despite the collapse of the Roman Empire in those areas. He could not not speak what he had seen and heard.

• Ambrose of Milan resisted the demands of the Empress Justina that he turn over the Portian Basilica in Milan to Arian Christians. "Take whatever is mine," he said. "My property, my life. But the Church is not mine to give." His refusal to yield rallied the people of Milan, who packed the church and refused to budge. The Empress had to give up her demands. Ambrose could not not speak what he had seen and heard.

• Martin Luther at Worms refused to recant what he had written in twenty-five pamphlets, notwithstanding almost certain death for his refusal. "Unless I am convicted by that or by right reason (for I trust neither in popes nor in councils, since they have often erred and contradicted themselves)—unless I am thus convinced, I am bound by the texts of the Bible, my conscience is captive to the Word of God, I neither can nor will recant anything, since it is neither right nor safe to act against conscience. God help me. Amen." He could not not speak what he had seen and heard.

## Why So Compelling?

What is so compelling about this Word that people, ordinary people, will give their very lives for it? Surely the answer does not lie in rational logic, which might compel a Socrates to die for a great cause. This Word does not come as a logical syllogism that human reason cannot resist. "My speech and my proclamation," the Apostle Paul confessed, "were not with plausible words of wisdom, but with a demonstration of the Spirit and of power" (1 Cor 2:4-5).

From the first, this logic-defying message of Christ crucified has evoked ridicule and rejection. It was, Paul confessed, "a stumbling block to Jews and foolishness to Gentiles" (1 Cor 1:23). As much as he admired Christian martyrs, the Stoic emperor/philosopher Marcus Aurelius found it mind boggling that Christians acted as they did on the basis of what he thought was an utterly irrational message. So too did the famous physician Galen and hundreds more.

The clue to our poser would appear to reside in the words "what we have seen and heard." The "boldness" of unlearned and unlettered people stemmed from the fact that they "recognized them as companions of Jesus" (Acts 4:13), the Word. The message that motivated and emboldened them was one they had experienced, "Christ, the power of God and the wisdom of God" (1 Cor 1:24). The message that motivated and emboldened them was an embodied and enfleshed message: "God loves you."

No one I know of grasped the truth of the power of the Word of God better than Martin Luther. When radical reformers threatened to scuttle the reform in Wittenberg by violence, Luther appealed to his followers to let the Word do its work. He pleaded with those who wanted immediately to abolish the mass and a lot of other things not to force the matter by dragging people away from it by force. "The matter should be left to God; His word should do the work alone, without our work." Why? Because God alone can effect faith in the heart that would enable people to forsake the mass and trust Christ. "In conclusion," declared Luther, "I will preach it, teach it, write it, but I will constrain no man by force, for faith must come freely without compulsion." The reason: Because of the Word, he did not have to use force. "I simply taught, preached, and wrote God's Word; otherwise I did nothing. And then while I slept, or drank Wittenberg beer with my Philip and with Amsdorf, the Word so greatly weakened the papacy, that never a prince or emperor inflicted such damage upon it. I did nothing; the Word did it all."

Luther incorporated the same insight into his great hymn "A Mighty Fortress."

The Prince of Darkness grim—
   We tremble not for him;
His rage we can endure,
   For lo, his doom is sure,
One little word shall fell him.

That word above all earthly powers,
   No thanks to them, abideth:
The Spirit and the gift are ours
   Thro' Him who with us sideth:

Let goods and kindred go,
   This mortal life also;
The body they may kill:
   God's truth abideth still,
His kingdom is forever.

## Confidence in the Word Today?

So Luther. But what about us? What about the Word in our world? Can we have confidence in the Word? Dare we stand back, as Luther pleaded, and let the Word work? Dare we preach it and teach it and go to bed or drink our beer or soft drinks with conviction that the Word is at work?

Judging by the frantic activity to the point of violence in our world, even in our religious world, I think we will have to conclude that many people—many Christians included—would say no to all of these questions. To be sure, we sing "A Mighty Fortress," but we often deny by our deeds what we say with our lips. We say, "If we don't do it with our earthly powers, it won't get done at all." In consequence, I fear, at every level of life, we live frantic, frenetic, violence-prone lives.

Don't hear this as a call for passivity: "Sit back! Stand around! Take no initiative!" The Word works through us. God has equipped us to think and to speak and to act. The question is whether we will think, speak, and act only on our own initiative or at the initiative of the Word and whether our thinking, speaking, and acting will not increase in wisdom, cogency, and power if we do.

Thomas Merton concluded that the reason violence has become endemic in western society is because modern persons no longer seek wisdom for its own sake, the Word of God. We seek, rather, the quickest way to solve problems, the violent way, which, in the long run, leaves larger problems than it solves. We need to learn how to wait for the Word to work, both corporately and individually, in matters both small and large.

I've been wondering: Was it the Word at work in Eastern Europe the past few decades that has effected something so utterly unexpected in the Soviet Union, Poland, East Germany, Czechoslovakia, Hungary, Romania, Bulgaria, and Yugoslavia? Georgie Ann Geyer, a political analyst, ascribed what happened in East Germany to the Lutheran Church. We can only judge in faith, but I am convinced that the peace movement in the churches, a product of the Word, has played a central role in all of this. More broadly, the Word, God's power, has been at work reordering history.

The Word is a word of peace. Christ is our peace, Paul says. He has broken down the dividing wall separating the peoples of the earth. He has made us all one—eastern and western, northern and southern. The Word has been at work.

The Word is a word of freedom. Christ has set you free, Paul says. He has set you free from whatever holds you fast: sin and the law. He has set you free for whatever God intends: love and justice and goodness. Let every tyrant quiver. Let every tyranny quake. The Word has been at work.

The Word is a word of human dignity and justice. Christ is God's righteousness. The Cross stands in judgment over every violation of human dignity. Agape declares every human life of infinite value. The Word has been at work.

What many persons doubt in the civil arena, however, many doubt also in the church arena. It goes like this, "We cannot trust the Word to work in people's lives. Rather, we must use our cleverness and all the powers at our disposal to effect conversions and to assure right faith and doctrine."

Once again, do not hear me contending for passivity. Two hundred years ago, Baptists fought a fierce battle over the use of means to effect conversions. Hyper-Calvinists, believing God has predetermined everything, opposed organized effort for missions. "If God wants people in Asia or Africa converted, God will do it all by Himself without any help from us." William Carey helped British Baptists break the stranglehold of that thinking in "An Enquiry into the Use of Means for the Conversion of the Heathen." The Great Awakening and frontier revival forced American Baptists to recognize the appropriateness of efforts to spread the good news.

Now we must ask, however, whether some, especially some Southern Baptists, have not become so confident in human instrumentality that they have forgotten or no longer have confidence in the Word. I raise this question along two lines:

Have some become so confident in human instrumentality that gimmicks substitute for genuine commitment to Christ as the end justifies any means? Is the Word at work in any way where—as Kierkegaard warned—variety and great moments, the reward motive, or the fear motive are used as the major means to manipulate?

The other question is more serious still. Have some become so confident in human instrumentality that they must impose their theological outlook on all and stop every word that does not conform to their stereotype? Is the Word at work in any way, as the Apostles pointed out here and as our Baptist forbears reiterated again and again, where obedience is coerced and where faith is not free?

The answer to both questions may not be absolutely clear, but I think it is quite clear that some Southern Baptists have little confidence in the Word of God's ability to transform the lives of people and to mold and shape their thought. Like the medieval inquisitors, they are convinced that they, rather than the Word, bear the heavy burden of assuring right faith. Their assumption is a vote of "no confidence" in the Word.

What we doubt in the civil and churchly arenas, we doubt also in individual arenas. We crowd our calendars with appointments and race frantically through them. We are anxious and worried about everything. We substitute quantity of activity for quality of life.

The Word speaks: "Do not worry about anything, but in everything by prayer and supplication with thanksgiving let your requests be make known to God. And the peace of God, which surpasses all understanding, will guard your hearts and your minds in Christ Jesus." (Phil 4:6-7). But do we hear? Do we respond? By our lives we say no all too often.

In 1991 Americans observed the two hundredth anniversary of the ratification of the Bill of Rights, the first ten amendments to their Constitution. In a very real way the First Amendment, "Congress shall make no law respecting an establishment of religion, nor prohibiting the free exercise thereof," is predicated on the conviction that the Word of God, if left free, can do far more to bring people to God than all the systems of coercion human beings ever devised. Religious liberty is a vote of confidence in the power of the Word. The vitality of religion in America gives powerful testimony that there is hope for the 1990s in the Word of God.

# Prayer

For littleness of faith in your Word, O God,
>      forgive us.
For imagining that our word is enough,
>           that our word can enlighten,
>           that our  word can transform,
>           that our word can bring order,
>      forgive us.
In this moment and in this place, O God,
>      we pray
>      For ears to hear not our words but yours,
>      For eyes to see your Word at work
>           in our world,
>      For minds to comprehend the message
>           of the Word to our day,
>      For wills compliant to the bidding
>           of the Word.
Above all, may we too have the courage
>      to tell what we have seen and heard.
>      Through Jesus Christ, your Word to us. Amen.

# The Salt of the Earth

## *Frank Stagg*

"You are the salt of the earth; but if salt has lost its taste, how can its saltiness be restored? It is no longer good for anything, but is thrown out and trampled under foot.

"You are the light of the world. A city built on a hill cannot be hid. No one after lighting a lamp puts it under the bushel basket, but on the lampstand, and it gives light to all in the house. In the same way, let your light shine before others, so that they may see your good works and give glory to your Father in heaven." (Matt 5:13-16)

## Introduction

Few biblical texts, if any, are more widely quoted than Matthew's "You are the salt of the earth"; but precisely what did it *intend*? What this or any text intended and what we hear it saying are not necessarily the same.

Along with the question of a text's intention is that of hermeneutics, method of interpretation. How do we go about seeking the intention of this or any biblical text? Related to the hermeneutical question are its implications for the nature of the Bible, its human limits as well as its divine inspiration. These are the concerns of this sermon: (1) What was intended by "You are the salt of the earth"; (2) How do we get behind the words of the text to its intention; and (3) What vision of the Bible does a sound hermeneutic give us?

Since my childhood, this text suggested something precise. I thought of "the salt of the earth" in terms of specific persons in my home church and community. These were unpretentious people, quiet and humble, marked by devotion and integrity, models morally and ethically, on the side of righteousness and justice. They were mature, not novices but tried and proven. They were faithful in the life and work of the church, but I knew that even hypocrites could pass such external tests. What these persons *were* and not just what they said or did showed them to be "the salt of the earth."

How did I come to this understanding? Probably I simply inherited it from others around me, not through scholarly study of the Bible or an informed hermeneutic. In retrospect, this early understanding seems basically sound. In part it attests to Luther's claim that the Bible is *algemeinverstaendlich*, commonly understandable, not limited to scholars or church "rulers."

After more than six decades of biblical study, I have more respect for the work of the specialists in hermeneutics; and I have been driven to a vision of the Bible as including human limits as well as divine initiative. Understanding the intention of a text belongs to the work of us all, laypersons and scholars working together. As Augustine said, "In this school, we are all fellow-disciples." Texts do not always have to be decoded in the study, but a sound hermeneutic has a necessary place.

## Salt: Its Uses and Metaphorical Usages

In what sense is one "the salt of the earth?" Context clearly implies that the text intends something good. Parallels in Mark 9:50 and Luke 14:34 are explicit: "Salt is good!" They do not say precisely how. All three synoptics link seasoning with salt. All three declare that "salt-less" or "insipid" salt can only be rejected and despised as worthless.

Matthew links the metaphor of "salt" with that of "light" (5:14-16), both metaphors defining the identity and vocation of the followers of Jesus. Both imply that ministry is inherent in salvation. Persons like those characterized in the Beatitudes are those whose nature and vocation is to relate redemptively to all people ("the earth" and "the world" themselves metaphors for "the people" of the earth or world).

Already in the earlier Gospel of Mark and followed by Luke appears not only the metaphor of "salt" but also of "light" (Mark 8:22-23; Luke 8:16-18); in these two Gospels, however, the metaphors are *not* joined as in Matthew.

Matthew joins the two metaphors, seemingly adapted from Mark, dropping Mark's "For everyone will be salted with fire" and the admonition, "Have salt in yourselves, and be at peace with one another." Why Matthew dropped these powerful texts is uncertain.

"Salted with fire" probably alludes to the Jewish practice of adding salt to a sacrifice or sealing a covenant with salt. With the probable reference to persecution, Mark puts "fire" in the place of salt, as in "fiery trials." Surprisingly, in 9:48 is the warning about the unquenchable "fire" of Gehenna! Does the Markan text intend to warn that Jesus' disciples will suffer fiery trials like the fires of Gehenna?

Mark's linking of "Have salt in yourselves" with being "at peace with one another," although not explicit in Matthew, may be implied as belonging to the vocation of people of the Beatitudes as being "the salt of the earth." To Matthew, Jesus' disciples are to be prophetic to the world, proclaiming the Law that exceeds the righteousness of scribes and Pharisees; and they are to be at peace with one another.

To cite a major variant, to Mark "salt" is something disciples are to "have." To Matthew, Jesus' disciples "are" the "salt." It probably was to make room for this emphasis on *being* that Mark's "Have salt in yourselves, and be at peace with one another" was omitted.

Lesser differences in Mark 9:50, Matthew 5:13, and Luke 14:34 appear in word selection and style, with the same basic intention. Mark writes, "But if the salt has lost its saltiness, how can you season it?" Matthew writes, "But if salt has lost its taste, how can its saltiness be restored?" Luke has verbal parallels and variants from Mark and Matthew.

What does Matthew's apparent redaction of Mark imply for the hermeneutical quest for the intention of our text and for a proper vision of the Bible? It implies that for the text before us we may find helpful clues in Mark and elsewhere, but ultimately we must seek Matthew's own intention, however like or unlike that in Mark. Redaction as in Matthew means also that the words of the Bible were not divinely dictated and that such terms as "inerrancy," "infallible," and "perfect" are derived from theological bias and not from the Bible itself. For Baptists historically, the Bible stands under no creed or council but is to be understood in terms of its own nature, content, and manner.

We are left with the question, In what sense are we "the salt of the earth"? The answer does not derive from etymology of the word "salt," whether in English, Greek, or Hebrew. Nothing inherent in the term or in salt itself tells us the intention of Jesus or Matthew. Since Matthew seemingly redacts Mark, his intention is not necessarily that of Mark. Context here and in Mark 9:50 and Luke 14:34f imply seasoning as the primary reference, but other usages of salt may be implied, as the use of salt in sacrifices and in covenants.

The basic hermeneutical clue is *usage*. Words do not have meaning; they have usage. Any word is a symbol, a vehicle that may carry intention. Communication takes place when speaker and hearer or writer and reader use words with the same or similar understanding.

In biblical interpretation, the task is to get behind the words of the Bible to the Word of God lurking there.

The same word may carry different intentions as context varies. A biblical example is "world" (*kosmos*), which has no single or inherent meaning. God loved "the world" (John 3:16); but we are *not* to love "the world" (1 John 2:15). Obviously, "world" is used in different ways in these texts.

In the perspective of Mark 9:50 and Luke 14:34, "salt is good," each thinking of salt as making food tasty. Within the narrow limits of the evangelists' concern, their proposition is valid. "Salt" that is "saltless" (Mark) or "tasteless" (Luke) is worthless and a hopeless anomaly.

Although the anomaly can be explained in terms of the mixture of "salt" taken from the seashore (NaCl plus other substances), this is not necessarily the solution. What may be intended is the absurdity of "saltless salt" or "tasteless salt," the metaphor being a caricature as in "the log in your own eye" (Matt 7:3f) and a camel going "through the eye of a needle" (Matt 19:24). These absurdities are not to be explained or explained away. Saltless or insipid salt and light that does not shine (Matt 5:14-16) are absurdities.

Seeking our text's intention is not simplified by a study of salt itself, its nature and functions. In fact, such study complicates the problem of textual interpretation. Salt may be "bad" or "good." Salt may be friend or foe, positive or negative. It may preserve or destroy. It may make food tasty or unsavory.

Scientifically, to be called "the salt of the earth" could be a compliment or indictment. The intention of our text is not to be derived from a scientific study of the function, behavior, or effects of salt. The intention of the text must be understood in terms of the ways the term "salt" was used in the time of Jesus and in particular by Matthew. Talk about the Bible as "scientifically inerrant" is a disservice to the Bible itself.

As a salt-water fisherman, I know salt as good and bad. It is indispensable to such game fish as speckled trout, redfish, flounder, or Spanish mackerel. Heavy rains along the coast can so reduce the salinity of the Mississippi Sound, where I fish, that the fish move out deeper into the Sound. No salt, no fish!

I also transport a boat on a drive-on trailer, having to back the trailer into the water to launch or load the boat. Salt water corrodes metal. Most of the trailer is galvanized, so resistant to corrosion; but even such a trailer has some metal that can be eaten up by salt water.

The vehicle used to tow the boat is vulnerable to corrosion, even if undercoated. Thus, salt is my friend as a fisherman but my enemy as a boatman. There is nothing inherent about salt that makes it good or bad, preserver or destroyer. Salt behaves in the pattern of "situational ethics!"

To diet-sensitive people today, salt is a problem, a threat to health —something not considered by our text. To me personally, salt raises the specter of tinnitus. This was not in my perception of salt until thirteen months of commuting from Mobile to Greenville, South Carolina, each weekend while serving as interim pulpit minister for First Baptist, Greenville. Passengers were served no meals, but each person was given two bags of salted peanuts on each lap of the flight, Mobile to Atlanta, next to Greenville, and the same returning. Eight bags of peanuts each weekend upset my otherwise careful diet. Ringing became roaring, driving me in desperation to an otologist. He diagnosed the problem as too much sodium, causing a fluid buildup in the cochlea! He prescribed a rigid low-sodium diet and soon the tinnitus was gone, with no impairment to the taste once the right recipes were found. Our text did not address this negative force of salt.

What then does our scientific knowledge of salt as corrosive and a threat to health do for our text? It reminds us that words have usage, not meaning. It reminds us that language is more poetry than science. It reminds us that the hermeneutical task is to seek to understand the intention of a text and the limits under which it was given. To take biblical language seriously, it must be taken intentionally, not literally.

## Salt and Biblical Usage

When the term "salt" was used in our text, salt was a normal household commodity, seen as essential to life. Salt was so essential that it was a part of a Roman soldier's pay, hence our tern "salary," the *sal* in salary being from the Greek word for salt (*hals=sals*). To be "worth one's salt" was to be worth one's salary.

That salt was seen as indispensable to food is attested by Job 6:6, "Can that which is tasteless be eaten without salt?" Job knew nothing of a salt-free diet. This limited usage of salt as seasoning is explicit in Matthew 5:13, Mark 9:50, and Luke 14:34f.

Salt also was used as a preservative for meat, a practice that continued throughout my boyhood. Fresh meat could be smoked or salted down. In such usage, salt was good. Along with its expressed function of seasoning food, our text probably also perceived salt as a preservative, but this is not explicit.

That our understanding of salt varies from the biblical one does not invalidate the *intention* of the text, but it does require that we understand how salt was then perceived and how the term was used at a given time. To take a text "as it is" requires that we understand "how it was."

We do have evidence as to ways salt was used or perceived in biblical times other than for seasoning and as a preservative. Elisha is said to have used salt to sweeten a foul spring at Jericho (2 Kgs 2:20-21). Salt could be used as fertilizer (Luke 14:34-35), or it could render land barren (Deut 29:23; Judg 9:45; Jer 17:6; Zeph 2:9). Thus, even in biblical perspective, salt does not bear an unambiguous or consistent role, compelling hermeneutics to inquire for *intention*, not inherent meaning.

More important to the intention of our text is the ancient practice of using salt in connection with sacrifices (Exod 30:35; Lev 2:13; Ezek 43:24) and with covenants (Num 18:19; 2 Chron 13:5; Lev 2:13). A "covenant of salt" seems to imply the integrity proper to the bonds within a covenant. An Arab phrase, "there is salt between us," seems to imply covenant bonds not to be broken; and a Persian phrase *namak haram*, "untrue to salt" (*Britannica*, "Salt"), seems to reflect the same usage of salt in sealing a covenant. Thus, behind our Matthean text may be a covenantal idea, with emphasis upon fidelity. Followers of Jesus are supposed to be in covenant with him and with one another, a covenant not to be broken or betrayed.

Neither Mark nor Luke has Matthew's "You are the salt of the earth," but both have a positive perception of salt. Mark 9:49 reads, "Salt is good; but if the salt becomes saltless, with what will you season it?"; Luke 14:34 has it, "Salt is good, but if the salt becomes tasteless, with what will it be seasoned?" (my translation). The nature of the "good" is not stated, but the saltless "salt" is "fit neither for the soil nor for the manure pile; they throw it away" (Luke 14:35). However "saltless" or "insipid" salt is to be understood, the three Synoptics expose the worthlessness of sham, a fatal anomaly in religion.

Mark's closing comment on salt may come closest as a clue to the intention of the Matthean text, "You are the salt of the earth." Mark has it, "Have salt in yourselves, and be at peace with one another" (9:50b). The peace implied may be the peace within covenant relationship, sealed with salt and kept faithfully. Why Matthew omitted this is a puzzle. Possibly it was to make room for the perception of disciples as themselves "the salt of the earth," not just possessors of it.

Similar to Mark is Paul's injunction, "Let your speech always be gracious, seasoned with salt, so that you may know how you ought to answer everyone" (Col 4:6). This implies that we are to be gracious to one another in covenant relationship and also to respond to all people appropriately and in keeping with who and what we are as followers of Jesus Christ.

## Priority of Being over Saying and Doing

Jesus said, "Ye *are* the salt of the earth." He thus spoke of *being* as primary. Saying and doing may be significant, or they may be empty or hypocritical. Jesus warned against saying "Lord, Lord" but not obeying. He warned against hearing without heeding, like building on sand. He demanded obedience and compliance, yet he warned that doing even mighty deeds may be nothing more than meaningless performance (Matt 7:21-27).

It is *what we are* that gives value to what we say or do. Creeds, however correct or competent, may be recited meaningfully or not. We may do good and yet be nothing more than "do gooders." For example, there are kind people, but no words inherently are kind and no actions inherently are good. Identical words may be kind or unkind. So with actions. A shove is in itself neither kind nor unkind. If we shove in anger or to hurt, the action is evil. If we shove another out of the path of danger, shoving is good, possibly heroic.

Jesus declared that we *are* the salt of the earth and the light of the world. Salt has its own agenda. It does not decide to function in a certain way; it is programmed to do so. So it is with light. To be light is to give light. Thus, the basic ministry of a follower of Jesus is simply *to be* what one is.

## Conclusion

In the time of Jesus, salt was so universally perceived as necessary to life that, as a metaphor and without decoding, it communicated to

Jesus' hearers the vocation belonging inherently to them. What salt was to the "earth" (people in all the earth), Jesus' followers were to be in ministry to all people.

As seen already, only one property or function of salt is explicit in our text, that of seasoning. The focus is on our *being* "salt" and being that *authentically*. Surely we are called to be more than "seasoning." The text may deliberately refrain from a fuller delineation of the function of salt, thus a pregnant text open to other ways in which salt is serviceable: preserving, sacrificial service, binding covenant, or more.

"You" (plural) is emphatic in the Greek text, probably looking back to those described in the Beatitudes. Just such ones as these are "the salt of the earth." These are the seemingly powerless, the poor in spirit, those who mourn, the meek, those who hunger and thirst for righteousness, the merciful, the pure in heart, the peacemakers, and the persecuted. They are like the prophets, whose function is to hear the word of God and proclaim it to the world, in particular to the power figures and structures of the world, that power may serve people and not enslave or debase them.

The vocation of "the salt of the earth" is implied in the sermon that followed about the righteousness that exceeds that of the scribes and Pharisees (Matt 5:17-20). Such persons as appear in the Beatitudes have as their vocation both embodying and living out the Law that Jesus came to fulfill. Their good works as salt and light are not to be self-serving but for the glory of God.

# The Demand
# beyond the Commands

## *Paul S. Fiddes*

After this there was a festival of the Jews, and Jesus went up to Jerusalem.

Now in Jerusalem by the Sheep Gate there is a pool, called in Hebrew Beth-zatha, which has five porticoes. In these lay many invalids —blind, lame, and paralyzed. One man was there who had been ill for thirty-eight years. When Jesus saw him lying there and knew that he had been there a long time, he said to him, "Do you want to be made well?" The sick man answered him, "Sir, I have no one to put me into the pool when the water is stirred up; and while I am making my way, someone else steps down ahead of me." Jesus said to him, "Stand up, take your mat and walk." At once the man was made well, and he took up his mat and began to walk.

Now that day was a sabbath. So the Jews said to the man who had been cured, "It is the sabbath; it is not lawful for you to carry your mat." But he answered them, "The man who made me well said to me, 'Take up your mat and walk.' " They asked him, "Who is the man who said to you, 'Take it up and walk'?" Now the man who had been healed did not know who it was, for Jesus had disappeared in the crowd that was there. Later Jesus found him in the temple and said to him, "See, you have been made well! Do not sin any more, so that nothing worse happens to you." The man went away and told the Jews that it was Jesus who had made him well. Therefore the Jews started persecuting Jesus, because he was doing such things on the sabbath. But Jesus answered them, "My Father is still working, and I also am working." For this reason the Jews were seeking all the more to kill him, because he was not only breaking the sabbath, but was also calling God his own Father, thereby making himself equal to God.

Jesus said to them, "Very truly, I tell you, the Son can do nothing on his own, but only what he sees the Father doing; for whatever the Father does, the Son does likewise. The Father loves the Son and shows him all that he himself is doing; and he will show him greater works than these, so that you will be astonished." (John 5:1-21)

"You search the scriptures because you think that in them you have eternal life; and it is they that testify on my behalf. Yet you refuse to come to me to have life. I do not accept glory from human beings. But

> I know that you do not have the love of God in you. I have come in my
> Father's name, and you do not accept me; if another comes in his own
> name, you will accept him. How can you believe when you accept glory
> from one another and do not seek the glory that comes from the one
> who alone is God? Do not think that I will accuse you before the Father;
> your accuser is Moses, on whom you have set your hope. If you believed
> Moses, you would believe me, for he wrote about me. But if you do not
> believe what he wrote, how will you believe what I say?" (John 5:39-47)

A little while ago I read in my daily newspaper about three public-
spirited men who witnessed a youth mugging an elderly woman,
punching and kicking her as she lay on the ground. They chased after
him, and in an effort to escape them the youth ran into a railway
station (East Putney) and onto a platform. The men who were pur-
suing him tried to follow, but were stopped at the barrier by the
ticket-collector because they had no tickets. They explained what had
happened, but the railman on duty was adamant—no tickets, no
entry. Could they use the phone in his office to call the police, then?
Certainly not was the reply; the booking office was closed. What
could they do? Finally they bought platform tickets, and only then
were they allowed to go onto the platform, catch the mugger, and
find a public telephone box to call the police. The judge who tried the
case at The Old Bailey, Mr. Justice Melford Stevenson, sentenced the
youth to five years in prison and then added that "the incident should
be brought to the notice of the railway authorities."

As I thought about this story, it seemed that the ticket collector
was not able to go beyond his book of rules, beyond the demands of
the railway laws. Faced with an unexpected situation, he fell back on
what he knew—the regulations. Perhaps he was uncertain about
whether he was being tricked or being made a fool of; so he played
safe and went by the rules. He was not able to respond freely to the
demand of the moment. That is the spirit of legalism: living by the
letter of the law and making the written law ultimate.

That mood of legalism is not only present in the everyday life of
our society; it is widespread in people's spiritual life, in their living
before God. It is easier to go by the rules, to "play by the book," than
to live freely and responsibly.

In our story from the Gospel quoted above, the Jewish religious
authorities were faced by an unexpected event. A man who had been
a cripple for thirty-eight years was up and about, walking around.
Confronted by this surprising witness to the power of God, they were
only able to fall back on the rules: they protested that he was carrying

his bed on the Sabbath day and so "working" on the day when nobody was supposed to work. He was shifting the furniture—even if only a rolled-up mat. When they discovered that he had been cured by Jesus, they fell back on the regulations once again; Jesus too had been working on the Sabbath day by healing the man and so could not possibly have God's approval for what he was doing. These religious people had been deeply challenged in their view of how the world is, and they met this challenge by playing safe, going by the law. They felt certain that "you are not allowed to carry your bed on the Sabbath."

Many years before, in the time of their great national leader Moses, God had indeed given his people the Ten Commandments for living, which included the command to keep the Sabbath as a holy day, free from work. We read in the book of Exodus:

> For in six days the Lord made heaven and earth, the sea, and all that is in them, but rested the seventh day; therefore the Lord blessed the sabbath day and consecrated it. (20:11).

This account, however, itself makes clear that the Sabbath was to be a day of release from the daily pressure of work in order to enter into God's own joy and satisfaction in the world God had made. What was really central to this command was a relationship of obedience to God and a sharing in creativity. This is true of all the commandments; beyond the particular command is the demand of God upon human life in our meeting with the divine. God has a purpose for our lives, and this is what is eternal and absolute. God knows what is best for us and what will make for fullness of life, and so God makes a demand upon us as the Creator who has a perfect will for His creatures. To help us find this purpose he gives us guidelines for living. At particular moments in human history God gave His people a commandment, suitable for their time and place. They heard the eternal demand in the form of a particular command. But these laws could only be an incomplete expression of God's eternal will for the people, a shadow of reality.

Jesus himself certainly believed that the laws of the past, even those recorded in the Old Testament scriptures, were not of utmost importance; what really mattered was God's will and purpose, and all moral and religious rules had to take second place to this. The commands given through Moses and the prophets were sign-posts not chains; they were principles but not prisons.

A paraphrase of our text tells us what mattered for Jesus in the end: "The Son does whatever he sees the Father doing." This is what Jesus said to his critics in this Gospel story. The true Son imitated his Father; he did what his Father does. Perhaps Jesus had a little picture in mind, the sort of homely scene he must have grown up with in Nazareth. A workman—a carpenter, for example, took his son into the workshop. The child saw his father planing a plank of wood, shaping a piece of furniture. The son learned his craft by watching his father. Standing there among the wood shavings, the son did what he saw the father doing.

Now, said Jesus, that is true of the heavenly Father. The obedient Son copied the Father in his works of love and healing. As for doing works of compassion on the Sabbath, Jesus pointed out that, "My Father is still working, and I also am working" (v.17). "God works on the Sabbath," Jesus said, "and I am copying him." The Jewish teachers had to admit that God always went on working. Though he had rested from his initial work of creation, they thought he could not have retired completely (to an eventide home, as it were), or else the whole world would fall apart. For instance, God still went on giving life and ending life with the summons of death. God was still the Lord of life and death; people were still being born and dying, even on the Sabbath.

So Jesus claimed that he must share in his Father's work of giving life—life in the deepest sense—not only the healing of bodies but the healing of the personality (John 5:21). Jesus offered the forgiveness of his Father to this man who was crippled in every way. He offered an entrance into God's family that needed no entrance ticket of keeping the rules; it required only a confession of need, repentance, a broken heart, and a contrite spirit.

Here was the clash between Jesus and the religious leaders of his time. In their uncertainties and anxieties they played safe; they simply went by the rules, by the letter of the law rather than by the spirit within it. Without the rule book they felt lost. But the result was that they had to build a massive system of little rules on top of the large ones, to make the rules fit every conceivable occasion. The Pharisees, for example, decreed that among 1500 other things that keeping the Sabbath day holy meant, it meant not wearing false teeth! The explosion of petty regulations like this finds its echo in the pronouncement of a seventeenth-century Scottish preacher that profaning the Lord's name included sleeping during the sermon!

If we live by the rules, then the rule book expands. We cannot live freely. This Gospel story of the healing on the Sabbath tells us that there is a Demand beyond the commands of the law, and first this is:

# The Demand of a Person

Jesus looked for the demand of God his Father, to which religious rules could only faintly point. "The Son does what he sees his Father doing." We, alas, cannot see the Father as clearly as Jesus could. We are not true, obedient sons as he was. But the glorious news of the gospel is that we can live in the Spirit of Jesus, and he reveals the Father. We may dare to add to these words of Jesus, and say, "What the son does, his brothers and sisters do also."

Later on in this Gospel record, Jesus says to us as his disciples, "This is my commandment, that you love one another as I have loved you" (John 15:12). We are set free to live according to God's demands upon our lives in a new way; we are obedient to a different kind of law, the law of love in the Spirit of Christ. Beyond the commands of the law is the demand of a person.

The Gospel writer underlined this by recording an important saying of Jesus immediately after this story of the healing of the crippled man, and immediately after the protests of those who lived just according to the rules. Jesus says:

> You search the scriptures because you think that in them you have eternal life; and it is they that testify on my behalf. (John 5:39)

Beyond the written code there is the demand of a Person, saying "come to me." Faced by the problems of our lives, not sure how to live as God's children in the world today, we must ask the questions "What would Jesus do?" and so, "What does Jesus want?" The loving thing to do, following the new command of love, is not just what we think is loving. It is God's demand of love, as unveiled in Christ. He alone knows what is best for our lives and others. Beyond the command of the law is the demand of a Person, the one who is supremely personal and utterly love.

But of course, the simple question "What would Jesus do?" is not an easy one to answer. Most of us need a lot of help in answering it, for we quickly fall out of tune with the Spirit of Jesus. First we need to soak our minds and hearts continually in the gospel story of Jesus, to meditate upon that witness to him in the scriptures. There is also a place for the commandments that God gave his people in the past which are recorded for us in Holy Scripture, and which express his purpose in a particular time and setting. They are not absolutes, but they are witness to which we must listen. We must take them seriously as sign-posts. They lay a prior claim upon us as we seek in our own day to hear God's demand. The way that the people of God heard the demand in the past cannot be ignored; we must have good reason to set these commands aside.

The love of Christ may indeed compel us in some situations to set the letter of the law on one side in order to get at the true spirit of God's demand, which is the demand of a Person. We will never do this lightly, however, and it will often be in anguish of heart. For example, the commandment as given through Moses says, "You shall not steal." Yet the love of a mother for a starving child may require her to steal bread to keep the child alive. The concern of a civil servant for the well-being of his country may prompt him to steal a document and send it to a newspaper, so that the public may know about the dishonesty of government. Who can doubt the pain that lies behind such decisions? These commands are sign-posts and not chains, but we would be foolish to ignore the signposts provided on our journey in favor of sheer blind instinct.

Something else too will help us to act in accord with the Spirit of Jesus and find the demand of the Person, something to which our Gospel story especially points. Faced with a hard decision about what we should do as a Christian, we need to take time to understand the situation we are in. The Jewish leaders in our story failed to see the healed man as he actually was. They were blind to his thirty-eight years of handicap, to all the limits he had to struggle with day by day; they did not think of him as a man who had lain beside a pool discarded, useless, and unwanted for the best part of his life. They did not see him at all, not the real person; all they could see was a man carrying a bed. All they noticed was the affront to their sense of what the rules were. People should not carry beds on the Sabbath, and this was a bed-carrier. Jesus, however, saw him as he was. He saw his physical disability, and he saw beyond it to the real needs of his spirit: "See, you have been made well!" he bid him, "Do not sin anymore" (John 5:14).

So if we are to ask, "What would Jesus do?" we must take time and effort to see into the situation as deeply as possible. We must review it in prayer, in company with Jesus and also use all the tools of our mind to understand it, with all the hard intellectual analysis we can muster. It is no easy thing, but hard work to ask, "What would Jesus do?"

Nearly twenty years ago now there was a strike in Britain among workers in the gas industry (strikes, I must add, are very rare indeed in present day Britain!). A Baptist minister wrote about this to one of our national newspapers, and his letter was published beneath a vivid picture of the East Greenwich Gasworks and a headline: "Gas Workers Dispute: What would Jesus do?" The minister wrote that he was full of anxiety about possible accidents in homes due to this industrial action, and commented, "Certainly those who have called for this action will have to carry the full moral responsibility for any injuries." Plaintively he went on, "As a Baptist minister I have never had an increase of anything like the £2.40 offered and have many times had to scrape the bottom of the barrel, but through the grace of God I have found a deep contentment in life that I would not want to exchange for anything." He concluded by appealing to the workers as well as to "the capitalists and shareholders . . . truly to repent of this national selfishness; let us make every issue a matter of prayer, asking 'What would Jesus do?' and within months . . . a new and happier spirit would fill the land." The next day another letter appeared, under the headline "Gospel Truths in Gas Dispute." It began like this:

> Sir—As a member of the Christian Brethren and branch secretary of a union, I found the minister's appeal to the Jesus Way sadly simplistic. I agree that trade unionists are just as prone to original sin as their capitalist masters; but the Jesus Way is not mere pietism. The Jesus of the Gospels would call a den of thieves just that.

It does not matter, at this distance of time, whether or not you agree with the second writer that the management bore some resemblance to a den of thieves. The basic point he was making is what is important. We need to look carefully and see what the situation really is, to understand its causes deep beneath the surface. We cannot speak vaguely of a spirit of peace and contentment, without asking why there is no peace, and what justice means.

If we are to get beyond the mere demands of the rules to the demand of a person, the demand of God itself, we must make sure that we are seeing things as they really are. That requires an investment of time and effort, and like all discipleship it is a costly matter.

Then we shall make a second discovery: beyond the commands of the law is:

## The Demand with No Limits Except Love

If we live by a rule book, then we try to find out how little we can get away with and still meet our obligations. Law tells us how much we have to do and no more. The way of the legalist is the way of the absolute minimum. We are prone to ask: "How much of the Bible do I have to read each week? How long do I have to spend thinking about this problem? How much do I have to give to this appeal for famine relief? How long do I have to spend talking to this rather unattractive person who shares none of my interests?"

The way of the law is the way of the minimum. If you or I were traveling behind a car and saw its back wheel wobbling, the traffic law in Britain would not require us to give the driver a warning hoot. In Britain, as in some American states, there is no Good Samaritan law. The law would have nothing to say to us if we overtook him to put as much space between us and a possible collision as soon as possible. That is the way of the strict letter of the law, and we can carry over that kind of approach into the life of the Spirit, asking only "What am I obliged to do? What is in the contract?"

But the demand of love maximizes. It asks not "What must I do?" but "What can I do?" It is this kind of spirit to which Jesus pointed when he spoke about the work of his Father, "My Father is still working, and I also am working." The Father persists in working for life and healing even on the Sabbath.

Now of course we cannot work flat out all the time, not even for God. We need rest; we need to know when we have reached our boundaries of health or energy. We need to have limits. What is important is how the limits get drawn. The attitude is what matters here. Does love draw the limits—love for others, love for God, and in a proper sense love for ourselves? Does love lay down the boundaries, or is it our insistence on our rights?

In the so-called "Sermon on the Mount" recorded in another Gospel, Jesus outlined a whole series of pictures of what it might look like to live according to the demands of God.

> If anyone strikes you on the right cheek, turn the other also; . . . if anyone wants to sue you and take your coat, give your cloak as well; . . . if

anyone forces you to go one mile, go also the second mile . . . give to
everyone who begs from you, and do not refuse anyone who wants to
borrow from you.
(Matt 5:39-42)

Jesus was not laying down a set of new laws here; he was greater
than Moses. If these sayings were rigid laws that had to be obeyed on
all occasions, then we would not always be acting in love and justice.
It does not help a tyrant if you never resist him; it does not help the
alcoholic on the street if you always give him money that he will
spend on drink.

So why did Jesus say these things? He was inviting us to look at
this picture, and at that. The kingdom of God may demand even this
of you, he was saying; you are not to draw the limits to what love
may demand. When the rule of God draws near, it may mean even
losing your shirt, your dignity, your preferences, your life. . . . Love
draws the limits, not we.

Beyond the commands of the law is a demand with no limits
except love. If we live in this spirit, it will be felt by others. A lot of
difference exists between only having twenty minutes to talk to someone who is lonely and spending those minutes looking at the clock
with our mind on the next thing we have to do. Love maximizes.

When someone has done something praiseworthy, it is so easy to
offer only the absolute minimum in terms of congratulation and encouragement; we have to say something, and we may take care not to
say too much because we are envious. When we need to apologize to
someone, we can do it grudgingly and formally, saying the least thing
we have to say within common decency; it is less painful to say,
"what a shame" than "I'm sorry." We may avoid actually accusing
someone of something we know is not true; we do not bear false witness, and yet we might let an innuendo about him circulate, because
we dislike him or her.

In all these ways we might take the path of the legal minimum,
but love maximizes. We can dare to live beyond the mere command
of the law and find the adventure of life in the spirit of Jesus.

Beyond the command of the law there is the demand of a person
and the demand with no limit but love. Finally, there is:

# The Demand for a Decision

You may notice that John the evangelist in telling his story did not give the crippled man a very good write-up. Even granted his handicap, the man appeared rather lethargic, unwilling to take any firm action to help himself. He grumbled about those who beat him in getting to the curative waters first and seemed to luxuriate in his grievance. Jesus had to face him with a demand for decision—"Do you want to be made well?"—and even then the man could not give him a straight answer. When he received healing, he let Jesus slip away without asking his name, and Jesus had to seek him out to challenge him with the next step in his life.

Living in the Spirit of Jesus means being ready to make choices. "Do you want to be made well?" "Do you want to leave your sinful ways?" Beyond the safety of rules and regulations we need to be able to respond to the challenge of the moment, to choose what seems right, to seize the opportunity, to take a risk.

Jesus affirmed that his Father is still working, always bringing life to the world. In the same way, the Son brings a moment of choice between life and death (John 5:21). When Jesus comes there is judgment, a call for response. This is true when we first put our faith in Christ as Lord, and it goes on being true in our lives as Christian disciples. To live is to choose. Beyond the security of the rules there is the step of adventure, to dare to stand up and walk.

It is easy to put off the steps we know we should take—the word we have to say to someone, the letter we have to write. Some people constantly shift their responsibility onto others; it is always the fault of someone else that they have not done what they wanted to achieve. They are the victims of life. God, they complain, never gave them a fair chance. God never gave them exact instructions, never told them exactly what to do, though they asked enough times.

Some people ask others what they should do because they cannot trust themselves to choose. Perhaps no one has ever trusted them, and they have lost confidence in themselves. They want some powerful personality (a pastor, perhaps), simply to lay down the law. Some people go around asking advice from many people, but not because they are really looking for guidance; they are already clear about what they want to do, but they want someone else to take the responsibility of recommending it. They go on consulting opinions until someone confirms their own wish. Then they can turn that advice into a rule and blame someone else if things go wrong.

Perhaps we can recognize ourselves here, afraid to take a step of adventure. This is what the railman in our newspaper story could not do, faced by his crisis. This is what the Jewish leaders in our Gospel story could not do, faced by their crisis. This is what the crippled man only just did, with the help of Christ.

So Jesus comes to us all now again, saying, "Do you want to be made well?" "Do you really want to seize the new life I offer you?" "Do you want to face up to this problem you have been putting off?"

Now is the time to start the adventure. There is no better time than this. Jesus says to you, "Stand up and walk."

# The Bible Is True

## Hardy Clemons

All scripture is inspired by God and is useful for teaching, for reproof, for correction, and for training in righteousness, so that everyone who belongs to God may be proficient, equipped for every good work. (2 Tim 3:16-17)

Recently my wife, Ardelle, and I were driving through Albemarle, North Carolina, and stopped to pick up a quick lunch. When the order was ready, the waitress rang up the tab. The digital numbers on the cash register read $6.66.

I could see the young waitress react. "I can't charge you that!" she said. "I'll have to charge you $6.65 or $6.67."

"In that case," I wise-cracked, "I have a recommendation."

"This is no laughing matter, Sir," she said. "Don't you know what that means?" Not waiting for me to answer, she told me: "666 is the mark of the beast in the Bible. This means that if you pay me $6.66 we could both have bad luck. God could get us!"

"I interpret the Bible differently than that," I said. "I don't think that 666 means that God is out to get people."

"Look, Mister," she said, in a most serious tone, "there *is* no interpretation. Either you believe the Bible or you don't!"

I handed her a five-dollar bill and two ones. She gave me back thirty-five cents. As Ardelle and I drove on down the road eating our hamburgers, we talked about what it means to believe the Bible. We recalled hearing a man say in a sermon: "I believe the Bible is true—all the way from 'In the beginning' . . . through the maps."

The Bible *is* true! I believe that! I have found it to be a "lamp to my feet and a light to my path" (Ps 119:105) for many years now. I have met God and been met by God again and again as I have read the pages of the Bible. Repeatedly God has given me instruction, encouragement, grace, wisdom, and forgiveness as I read the Bible. God has often led me by the truth of the Bible in making mid-course corrections in my life.

The Bible's word for these mid-course corrections is "repent." By means of the Spirit of God who inspired the writing of this Book—and who inspires us as we read the Book—I have received guidance and strength. I have been taught and inspired to submit my life to God.

I know the Bible is true! It helps me experience what Jesus called "the truth that makes us free." It gives me wisdom and courage to follow its light. I trust the validity of the Bible. I honor the authority of the Bible. I believe the Bible is true.

I also know that in an attempt to have "a high view of the Bible" some people make claims for the Bible that it does not make for itself. I find the recent attempt to improve on the biblical word "inspired" with the non-biblical word "inerrant" to be a false argument. It is not totally unlike the "my daddy can whip your daddy" argument that children still use to show their "superiority." They make claims for their fathers that are unnecessary and not in keeping with the father's design. Believing the Bible doesn't mean being a literalist who won't interpret the truth offered in scripture. I do not "believe the maps," for example. Those map-lines were not inspired by God. People drew the lines on their own.

The land of the Bible remains pretty much the same as it did in Abraham's or Jesus' day, but a map from their day will not serve as a sufficient guide today. The maps had to be revised. If I am to find my way, I must keep updating my awareness of these maps. Everyone admits that. We can't pick up a map Abraham used and discover what we need for travelling today unless we interpret it. The truth of that day must be translated to our day to be understood accurately.

The words of the Bible also must be interpreted. W. T. Conner, the great theologian from Southwestern Baptist Seminary used to say: "The Bible means what it means. It doesn't always mean what it says." To hear the Bible's message, we must sometimes look beneath what it says to discover what it actually means.

"The mountains and the hills before you shall burst into song, and all the trees of the field shall clap their hands" (Isa 55:12) is obviously not a statement of fact. It is a statement of truth. When Jesus said to his disciples, "Take, eat; this is my body" (Matt 26:26), he was not stating fact; he was announcing truth deeper than facts.

I want to affirm, therefore, that the Bible is true. The truth of the Bible is accurate and adequate to reveal God to human beings when we listen and follow. But, all the truth in the Bible is not the same kind of truth.

## Much of the Bible's Truth Is Factual

This kind of truth means what it says and says what it means. When the Bible says that Jesus became a human being, it means what it says: Jesus became an actual, limited, vulnerable human being.

Jesus needed to eat and rest. He got excited and also discouraged. He was sometimes lonely and afraid. He needed nurture from God and his friends. As a boy, he upset his mother. When he was struck or cut, he bruised or bled; and when they crucified him, he was actually dead. He was as dependent upon the power of God as we are. As Dorothy Sayers, the British theologian put it:

> For whatever reason God chose to make humans as they are—limited and suffering and subject to sorrows and death—God had the honesty and the courage to take the same medicine. Whatever game God is playing with creation, God has kept God's own rules and played fair.[1]

Jesus was also genuinely divine. He participated in what it actually means to be divine. He was "God coming to us in Christ to reconcile the world to God." To paraphrase the way Dorothy Sayers puts that truth: "Jesus revealed God as God is and human beings as God meant for us to be." As my friend Grady Nutt used to say: "That's worth a ponder."

When the Bible says that Jesus was human and that Jesus was divine, it is speaking truth. But this truth is more than factual. It goes beyond literal truth to spiritual truth. It goes beyond factual truth to personal truth, and beyond that to mystery.

We humans have much more skill with which to solve problems than we formerly did. We can assimilate facts. We can amass and utilize vast amounts of knowledge. But we must stand before spiritual mystery in humility and awe. We must kneel before such mystery in the worship of God. We dare not claim to know more of the truth than we do! We dare not be arrogant with reference to truth as though it belongs to us. We possess truth "in clay jars" (2 Cor 4:7), as Paul puts it. We do not own truth. Even Jesus did not say, "I have the truth." He said, "I *am* the truth."

This means that we can never stand before the truth of God like a prideful student who has mastered the multiplication tables, and say: "Look at me, Ma! Be impressed with how I've mastered the truth." My father-in-law, Pastor E. F. Hallock, once told me: "I started out to read the Bible through four times every year. I thought I would master it that way. But, I never mastered the Bible, although I read it completely through at least four times each year for decades. What happened was: God worked through the Bible to master me."

To understand God, I must never stand with pride before any truth I perceive. I must stand under the truth in reverence, knowing that God always knows me better than I know God. We may know God's truth in humility—but only in humility. We must not claim to know more than we know. We must not make claims that the Bible won't support.

Some things even Jesus didn't know; he had to learn them. Some truth was beyond his knowledge. He told his disciples that he didn't know when the end would come; only God the Father knows that.

As Luke tells us: "And Jesus increased in wisdom and in years, and in divine and human favor" (Luke 2:52). Jesus lived his life in humility and courageous dependence upon God the Father. As he followed God, Jesus learned, grew, and developed—physically, intellectually, emotionally, and spiritually.

## Some Bible Truth Is Deeper Than Factual

Facts are true, but not all truth is fact. Some of the deepest truth in the Bible is not meant to be taken literally. This kind of truth includes a mystery that we can adequately approach only in reverence. We do not own God's truth. We do not possess it in our human hands. We have it, as the Apostle Paul says, "in clay jars, so that it may be made clear that this extraordinary power belongs to God and does not come from us" (2 Cor 4:7). God keeps me reminded that God is God and I am not. I think that this is what Paul meant when he said, "We walk by faith, not by sight" (2 Cor 5:7).

Much of the Bible's truth is metaphorical. When the Bible says, "The Lord is my shepherd," it is obviously not speaking literal fact; it is using pictures. The truth revealed in this great Psalm is: God relates to us as a shepherd relates to his sheep. God leads us, provides for us, nurtures us, and shows continuing compassion for us. God loves us—even enough to die for us, as shepherds sometimes died for their sheep. God's love for us cherishes our best interests, our continuing development, and our present as well as our ultimate well-being.

God corrects us, restores us, and renews us. It is true! God *does* lead us beside still waters! God *does* lead us into green pastures!

Sometimes the Bible speaks in parables. We Western, left-brained folks have a good deal of trouble with this Eastern, right-brained approach to presenting truth. Not many persons ask for the address and zip code of the prodigal son Jesus talked about. We know him and his elder brother all to well; unless, that is, we are so caught up in the literalism and legalism of the Pharisees that we dodge truth by overfocusing on facts. We know that Jesus was talking about us as much as he was a man who had two sons.

In Genesis 1-11 the Bible teaches us more about the who of creation than about its hows and whys. The "facts" of the creation story in chapter one don't fit with the "facts" of the creation story in chapter two. Chapter one speaks of male and female being created together, in the image of God, at the same time. Chapter two speaks of the male being created first, and then the female being created. The facts don't fit, but the truth fits when we are willing to hear it: God created the world, the first people, and us. God initiated life and graced us with what C. S. Lewis called "gift-love," so that we might experience and reflect the joy of God.

To try to interpret the story of the prodigal son or the creation from a factual viewpoint is to miss the truth offered to us through the inspiration of the scriptures. To argue about the length of the days or the age of the rocks is to miss the grace that is heralded by those ancient sages who heard the voice of God in the garden and came home from their own far countries to be greeted by the waiting Father whose prodigal love is the point of the story.

The Bible is one of the major ways God reveals truth for our human darkness. The Bible is capable of putting us in touch with the same God who inspired its authorship long ago. The Bible speaks God's word of creation and redemption to help us hear that these stories are not just factual accounts of the past; they tell our present stories too.

## The Bible's Truth Is Inspired

When the Bible speaks of itself in 2 Timothy, it says:

> All scripture is inspired by God and is useful for teaching, for reproof, for correction, and for training in righteousness. (3:16)

The Bible is saying that we have the gift of this matchless book because God "breathed it into creation." The word "inspired" means "breathed into" or "in-spirited" by God.

That's why Christians believe that the Bible is true, valid, valuable, authoritative for life, and adequate to put us in touch with God. That's why I believe it is not enough just to "believe the Bible," but that I must go beyond agreement to absorb and apply its truth to my life—and to our world. I must choose to see it and follow it as "a lamp to our feet and a light to our pathway." I must DO what it teaches. Only when I do the truth I am taught do I actually believe that the Bible is true!

As true as the Bible is, it is not the deepest level in the bedrock of our faith. The foundation of Christian faith is not the Bible. The ground of faith is God—God the Creator, God who comes to us in Jesus the Christ, God who inspires and energizes us through the Holy Spirit. God as Father, Son, and Spirit speaks to us in the words of the Bible. When I pick this book up and listen, I just may hear the Word of God.

As I heard the great preacher Sam Proctor remind us: "We had God a long time before we had a Bible." We don't believe in a book as much as we believe in God who inspired the writings. To over-focus on the book is to fall into idolatry—however well-meaning the effort. To read the book and become obedient to God who meets me in its pages is to be a person of genuine faith. To follow, to act in obedience, is to believe.

To say that believing in God is more foundational than believing in the Bible is not to have a "low view of the Bible." It is to have an accurate view of God! To believe that the Bible God inspired is true is to have an opportunity to hear this truth and to experience for yourself the God who speaks the living word to us.

Mary A. Lathbury in the old hymn says it as well as anyone:

> Beyond the sacred page
> I seek *thee*, Lord.
> My spirit pants for thee,
> O *Living* Word.

The word of God is spoken through persons—especially the Person of Jesus the Christ—more than it is through factual or theological or philosophical propositions. When we are discovered by such personal truth, which is genuinely revealed in the words of the Bible, we are indeed made free.

I believe the Bible is true! I am committed to read it regularly, to interpret it authentically—so that I may "rightly divide the word of truth." I am committed to follow its Lord and its truth faithfully.

I believe the Bible is true.

## Notes

[1]Dorothy L. Sayers, *Creed or Chaos: And Other Essays in Popular Theology* (London: Methuen & Co. Ltd., 1947) 2.

# Struggling for the Blessing

## *Elizabeth Barnes*

The same night he got up and took his two wives, his two maids, and his eleven children, and crossed the ford of the Jabbok. He took them and sent them across the stream, and likewise everything that he had. Jacob was left alone; and a man wrestled with him until daybreak. When the man saw that he did not prevail against Jacob, he struck him on the hip socket; and Jacob's hip was put out of joint as he wrestled with him. Then he said, "Let me go, for the day is breaking." But Jacob said, "I will not let you go, unless you bless me." So he said to him, "What is your name?" And he said, "Jacob." Then the man said, "You shall no longer be called Jacob, but Israel, for you have striven with God and with humans, and have prevailed." Then Jacob asked him, "Please tell me your name." But he said, "Why is it that you ask my name?" And there he blessed him. So Jacob called the place Peniel, saying, "For I have seen God face to face, and yet my life is preserved." The sun rose upon him as he passed Penuel, limping because of his hip. Therefore to this day the Israelites do not eat the thigh muscle that is on the hip socket, because he struck Jacob on the hip socket at the thigh muscle. (Gen 32:22-32)

Jesus, full of the Holy Spirit, returned from the Jordan and was led by the Spirit in the wilderness, where for forty days he was tempted by the devil. He ate nothing at all during those days, and when they were over, he was famished. The devil said to him, "If you are the Son of God, command this stone to become a loaf of bread." Jesus answered him, "It is written, 'One does not live by bread alone.' " Then the devil led him up and showed him in an instant all the kingdoms of the world. And the devil said to him, "To you I will give their glory and all this authority; for it has been given over to me, and I give it to anyone I please. If you, then, will worship me, it will all be yours." Jesus answered him, "It is written,

'Worship the Lord your God,
  and serve only him.' "

Then the devil took him to Jerusalem, and placed him on the pinnacle of the temple, saying to him, "If you are the Son of God, throw yourself down from here, for it is written,

'He will command his angels
　　concerning you,
　to protect you,'

and

'On their hands they will bear
　　you up,
　　so that you will not dash your
　　　foot against a stone.' "

Jesus answered him, "It is said, 'Do not put the Lord your God to the
test.' " When the devil had finished every test, he departed from him
until an opportune time. (Luke 4:1-13)

The following words are spoken by the Danish storyteller Isak
Dinesen in her autobiographical novel, *Out of Africa*: "My life, I will
not let you go except you bless me, but then I will let you go."[1]
Christians who know their Bible recognize her source. For Dinesen,
Jacob's struggle with the dark angel beside the Jabbok was the pattern
for her own dark struggles with disease, death, economic reversal,
and the conflicts within her own heart. Interlaced with the central
Christian story, that of Jesus of Nazareth, the Jacob story gave to
Dinesen, as it has for many others, a way to navigate the perilous
shoals of life and to arrive at the end of her journey blessed, albeit
wounded.

Look again at the Jacob story from the Genesis narrative printed
above. What do we find there? Struggle! Blessing! A new name!
Seeing God face to face! Striving with God and humans and prevailing! Brokenness and blessing! What does it all mean?

When William Faulkner received the Nobel Prize for Literature in
1950, he said something to the aspiring writers to whom he addressed
his remarks that helps to answer our questions. Faulkner advised
them not to write about this or that or the other good (not so good)
thing, but to write about the one thing finally worth writing about:
"the problems of the human heart in conflict with itself." Writing
about that universal struggle, the writer, Faulkner believed, would
attend to humanity's bedrock values themselves—"love and honor
and pity and pride and compassion and sacrifice."

The human heart in its conflict struggles toward these values. As
did Jacob beside the Jabbok, struggling with the guilty injury done to
his brother Esau so many years ago, we all wrestle with our sins, our

failures, the injuries done to us, dreams unrealized, opportunities ungrasped, sacrifices neglected, and pity unfelt and compassion unexpressed. Life is hard. We each hope to make it through life with a blessing in hand. Often, however, we confuse the blessing with something else. Our vision is limited and much competes for our attention, obscuring our view and confusing our perspective.

Jesus knew about this. Fresh from his baptism in the Jordan river, Jesus went into the wilderness and struggled for more than a night beside his own dark stream. Are we to suppose that Jesus easily turned away all the temptations beguiling him? That his struggle was a conflict in name only? Hardly! The narrative clearly tells us that the struggle was long, forty days long, and harrowing. Without food for the whole time, Jesus was weakened and "famished." The temptation to turn stone into bread was a strong one. Wealth and power were equally enticing allurements. How much easier it would have been to accomplish his goals with wealth and power to oil the machinery. Jesus' struggle was as perilous and demanding as Jacob's before him.

Like Jacob, too, Jesus could emerge with a blessing or a curse. He could emerge newly empowered to "bring good news to the poor . . . proclaim release to the captives . . . and recovery of sight to the blind, to let the oppressed go free, to proclaim the year of the Lord's favor" (Luke 4:18-19). This he did. But not without a fearsome struggle in the wilderness first, and not without emerging in some sense wounded and halt. Later, after a similar struggle in Gethsemane, Jesus would emerge again with the blessing, but this time at the ultimate cost of his life itself. His body broken and bleeding on the cross, Jesus would have striven with God and with humans and prevailed, and he would have seen God's face. He, too, would bear a new name—wonderful Counselor, almighty God, the Prince of Peace.

As Christians, those living the Jesus story today, we interlace the story of Jacob and the story of Jesus with our own stories, personally and corporately. We also have stood beside the Jabbok, trembling and afraid, and we have wrestled with those forces that would keep the blessing from us. As those who bear the name of Christ today, we have been led by the Spirit into our own wilderness, and we have prayed and labored in our dark Gethsemanes. The world's enticements of wealth and power have threatened to overwhelm us, and the suffering and setbacks of life have threatened to break our spirits.

Isak Dinesen's need for the encouragement and empowerment of the Jacob story and the Jesus story was, like ours, great. When she was ten, her father whom she loved dearly, committed suicide. In her twenties, she contracted syphilis from her husband and lost her capacity to bear children. After her divorce, she remained unmarried for the rest of her life and finally lost the man she loved in a plane crash. Faced with bankruptcy, she was forced to leave Kenya and the continent and people who had become home and family to her. Suffering daily with the pain and debilitation of advancing syphilis, Dinesen extracted the blessing from her struggle, becoming one of the world's extraordinary storytellers. Her stories, like her life itself, are stories of courage, compassion, and sacrifice. Finally, because her life had blessed her, she was able to let it go.

Today, the Christian church and, for our purposes, the Baptist community face multiple threats to their faithfulness as the body of Jesus Christ. Distorted interpretations of faith and the Bible by fundamentalists and the religious right, apathetic attitudes toward ecological irresponsibility and the plight of the earth, callous perspectives regarding the struggle of oppressed peoples to claim their full share of justice and the fruits of God's good creation, and the facile equation of extravagant economic wealth with God's providential care are modern temptations beguiling us to ignore the conflict that these enticements set up within our hearts.

Deep in our hearts, however, when we stand beside the Jabbok or find ourselves in the wilderness or kneeling in Gethsemane, we know that the blessing will not come until we have striven and prevailed against these errors. We will not see God's face and hear our names called new until we have struggled to free ourselves of these demonic forces and emerged blessed though halt. God's judgment on religious self-righteousness, the plunder of nature, injustice and hatred of our sisters and brothers, and the love of money and the things it can buy sounds the call to engage the battle beside the Jabbok. We are challenged by God's Holy Spirit to undertake the struggle. When we do, we will see the blessing, and we will see God's face.

But what does it mean to see God's face? Certain passages of scripture suggest (do they not?) that one cannot see God's face and live. The Jacob story claims that we *can* come face to face with God and live. In fact, it may well be that only if we *do* come face to face with God, we live—truly live. In many ways, only after Jacob (now Israel) emerged from his night's struggle with the dark angel, having looked into the face of God, was he finally ready to live fully. Only then did he feel true compassion for the brother he had deceived and cheated. Only then did he possess the courage to face Esau and the love to offer his service to him. Only then was Jacob ready to sacrifice himself for that which was more valuable than his own prosperity: compassion, courage, love, sacrifice—it sounds like Faulkner's list, does it not? The human heart in its own self-conflict struggles over these things—honor, integrity, compassion, justice, love, sacrifice, courage—and if it wins the struggle, these qualities are the blessing, the very aspect of God's own divine face.

As Baptists, we have read the stories of Jacob and Jesus and known them as our own. As twentieth century characters in the grand story of God's creative and redemptive story with Israel, Jesus, and the church, we live the story's latest enactment. So doing, we find ourselves responsible for new forms of faithfulness specific and unique to our day and time. God's Spirit moves out ahead and beckons us, "Come on, catch up." Only with the willingness to struggle and to emerge wounded will we be able to follow the Spirit's call. Today that divine call beckons us to find our faithfulness in places former generations of Christians never knew about—places of suffering where people die of new diseases like AIDS; mammoth, impersonal cities where hundreds sleep in the streets and eat from garbage cans; an earth with spoiled rivers and toxic air, eroded top-soil, and thousands of species of plants and animals made extinct by humankind's plunder of the creation.

As "people of the Book," Baptists own a vision of the Bible and its power that promises to engage the unique and difficult challenges of just this kind of world and its demand for new forms of Christian faithfulness. Interlacing our central story, the Jesus story, with our tragic stories of poverty, oppression, hunger, homelessness, overpopulation, ecological waste, violence, and our penchant for war and hatred over peace and lovingkindness, we hear our stories anew and find them transformed by the biblical story.

From the Bible we hear that things do not have to be as they are; they can be different; they can become faithful to God's beckoning toward wholeness, justice, plenty, and love. As those living most newly God's splendid story with Israel, Jesus, and the church, we are characters emboldened and energized by the Spirit of God to move out beyond our faithfulness and ennui, free from the stagnating elements around us and free to join God's Spirit in changing the conditions in which we have languished. Courage, passion, love, compassion, and self-sacrifice are called for and given by the Spirit.

We read the Bible and know that it is about us. We read the Bible and hear our names called and included in the list with Jacob, Abraham, Esther, Mary, Isaiah, Miriam, John, Lydia, Andrew, Joseph, and Tamar. We finally can see God's face with eyes newly opened by compassion for the homeless, pity for the ones dying of AIDS, courage to call injustice its real name, and sacrifice of privilege for connectedness to the earth and all its inhabitants human and para-human.

Struggling with the dark angel in modern-day forms, we, the people of God, refuse to turn loose until we, too, have looked into God's face and thereby found the strength and transformation needed to live life fully. When we finally prevail, however, as did Jacob we prevail because we have struggled mightily, ignoring exhaustion and terror for the worth of the struggle and the prize to be claimed. As did Jacob and Jesus, we emerge wounded and blessed. As did Jacob and Jesus, we have seen God's face and bear a new name.

Entering the world of the biblical text, Baptists have historically taken seriously their transformed status. Today, that status as "people of the Book" requires of us the same commitment it did of those who came before us; the goal is the same, but some new specifics have been added. Our faithfulness in this new day is promised the same help given those of old. God's own Spirit stands ready to engage the new challenges with us. Indeed, God's Spirit is already ahead of us. We do not have to break down the barriers alone. If we listen closely, we can hear the voice of the Spirit calling, "Come on, catch up."

## Note

[1]Isak Dinesen, *Out of Africa and Shadows on the Grass* (New York: Vintage, 1985) 287.

# Caution!

## *Charles E. Poole*

And no one puts new wine into old wineskins; otherwise the new wine will burst the skins and will be spilled, and the skins will be destroyed. But new wine must be put into fresh wineskins. And no one after drinking old wine desires new wine, but says, "The old is good." (Luke 5:37-39)

You search the scriptures because you think that in them you have eternal life; and it is they that testify on my behalf. (John 5:39)

But as for you, continue in what you have learned and firmly believed, knowing from whom you learned it, and how from childhood you have known the sacred writings that are able to instruct you for salvation through faith in Christ Jesus. All scripture is inspired by God and is useful for teaching, for reproof, for correction, and for training in righteousness, so that everyone who belongs to God may be proficient, equipped for every good work. (2 Tim 3:14-17)

## Introduction

"The Bible does perfectly what God intended for the Bible to do." I don't know if that sentence was original with Ben Philbeck or if he borrowed it, but in his mouth it made an enormous impression on my life.[1]

Ben Philbeck was my Old Testament professor at the old Southeastern Baptist Theological Seminary. He was my first professor. I didn't like him. I was an ardent, strident, opinionated young fundamentalist when I got off the bus in Wake Forest. I had decided not to let folks like Ben Philbeck "change me" or "ruin me." So I didn't like him . . . at first. By the time I left the place, I had figured out a few things, one of which was that the Ben Philbecks of this world are true and genuine followers of Jesus who love the Bible ardently and teach the Bible honestly.

Since those days long ago, the seminary (at least as I knew it) has passed away. So, tragically, has Ben Philbeck. He is gone from us now, taken from us much too soon by brain cancer. But that sentence of his still lives for me. It stirs around inside my mind whenever I think seriously about the sacred scriptures. "The Bible does perfectly what God intended for the Bible to do."

If we affirm that statement, then the next question must inevitably be, "And what, exactly, is it that God intended for the Bible to do?" As you might have suspected, I'm going to suggest that we will find the best answers to that question in the scripture passages printed above. In the passage from John we hear our Lord say that the scripture's purpose is to point us to Jesus who points us to God. In 2 Timothy, we hear the writer of that pastoral letter say that the purpose of scripture is to teach us the way of salvation and to equip us to live our lives as people of God.

That's about it. That's most of what the Bible says about the Bible. There's not a whole lot more in the scripture about the scripture. If I allow the Bible to define its own purpose, then I am left to say that God intended for the Bible to point us to Jesus, to show us the way to everlasting life, and to equip us to live in this world as people of God. And, yes, Professor Philbeck was right, the Bible does these things perfectly.

It is popular, these days, to suggest that God intended for the Bible to do other things. Some persons suggest that God intended for the Bible to be a science book or a world history book. They mean well. People who say those things have the best of intentions. We live in a culture that values objective facts and information so highly that people actually think they are paying the Bible a compliment when they say that the Bible's purpose is to serve as a compendium of scientific and historical facts. The Bible's purpose is higher and greater and other than that, however. The Bible's purpose transcends that of a collection of facts. The Bible's purpose is to hold before us the truth of God's goodness, grace, power, and love. The Bible's purpose is to point us to Christ and to equip us for life. That is what the Bible says about itself.

## Hearing the Bible Honestly, Taking the Bible Seriously

When you and I hear the Bible honestly and take the Bible seriously, then God uses the words in the Bible to point us to Christ, to show us hope and light for our most difficult trials, to challenge our self-centered ways and call us to follow Jesus in authentic discipleship, and to show us grace and forgiveness for our sin and guilt.

The Bible does perfectly what God intends for the Bible to do. Our scripture from 2 Timothy says that the Bible's purpose is to instruct us for salvation and to show us how to live in this world as people of God. If you and I hear the Bible honestly and take the Bible seriously, then the Bible fulfills those purposes powerfully, beautifully, even perfectly.

The Bible waits to be heard honestly and taken seriously. The Bible does not wait to be praised or defended; to be amended by the impertinent rationalism of inerrancy; to be complimented or adored; or to be used by those who have points to make, doctrines to defend, or debates to win. The Bible only waits to be heard honestly and taken seriously.

But be warned: If we hear the Bible honestly and take the Bible seriously, we will be changed. In fact, perhaps the word "caution" should be engraved on the fronts of Bibles. After all, if we aren't real careful, a Bible heard honestly and taken seriously might turn out to be more trouble than we bargained for.

No one has ever more fully captured the truth about a Bible heard honestly and taken seriously than the brilliant Fred Craddock, who said of the Bible:

> Live in the pages of this book, and it will cause you to be changed.
> Live in the pages of this book, and it will cause you to feel the razor edge of the moral demand of the Christian Gospel.
> Live in the pages of this book, and it will cause you to feel the vast distance between the sky of your intentions and the earth of your performance.
> Live in the pages of this book, and it will cause you to empty your pockets for someone else's children.[2]

Maybe we ought to have "caution" engraved on our Bibles—in little gold letters right beneath our names. A Bible can be a dangerous thing to have around. Of course, that's only if you live in its pages, hear it honestly, and take it seriously.

## Using the Bible to Avoid Change

Needless to say, many people who read the Bible a lot, who even study the Bible, are not changed. In fact, some people use the Bible to keep from having to change. If I come to the Bible with the notion that I will find authoritative words to back up my position and defend my opinions, then I can actually use the Bible to keep from changing. I can find a verse here and a verse there to endorse most any preconceived notion I might have. If I start with my ideas, my notions, and my opinions, then set out to find a verse that fits with my ideas, then I will not be changed by the scripture. Rather, I will use the scripture to defend and protect and sanction my own comfortable convictions.

If I use the Bible in such a way, then the Bible is a very comfortable book for me. It holds no danger. It never asks me to change. It never shows me anything new. It only reinforces whatever I already thought. If I use the Bible to support my ideas, then scripture, rather than becoming the challenge that leads me to change, becomes the fence I build around my unwillingness to change.

Most of us have learned that dreadful art of *using* the Bible. When we were children, we started our life with scripture by simply loving the Bible. We loved the wonderful stories. We learned early about Adam and Eve, Noah and the Ark, David and Goliath, Joseph and Mary, and the loaves and fishes. We felt the broad outlines of scripture that could be held by the handles of wonderful stories and familiar names. We just loved the Bible.

As adults, many of us began to learn the sad art of *using* the Bible. We start with an idea, opinion, tradition, or conviction with which we are comfortable and which we wish to defend. We then flip through the Bible as if it were a farmer's almanac for debaters until we find a verse that supports our opinion. "Ah-hah!" we exult when we discover that something in Leviticus or Titus or somewhere else backs up our pre-conceived notion about this or that critical issue. We have found an authority that endorses our position. We don't have to change. The Bible has come to our rescue!

For many people in the world that is the primary focus of their life with scripture. Their Bible has never once demanded them to change their ways. Indeed, they have learned to use their Bible as a defense against having to change because they can always find a verse to endorse whatever they are comfortable thinking or doing.

I learned that dreadful art early on in my life. I became rather proficient at using the Bible to defend, endorse, and support my preconceived notions with which I was comfortable. Across the years, however, by the grace of God, I have slowly unlearned that dreadful skill.

To "unlearn" a thing is more difficult than to learn a thing. Whatever it costs, however, whatever it takes, we must unlearn our skill at using the Bible so that we can learn to hear the scripture honestly, take the scripture seriously, and be changed by the hope and demand of the gospel that we find in the pages of scripture.

If you and I can set aside our inclination to use the Bible and if we, instead, will simply open our lives to hear the Bible, then we will be changed. If we honestly, openly, humbly live in the pages of scripture, we will be changed.

To say that we are changed by living in the pages of scripture is not to suggest that the Bible is some kind of lucky charm or magic wand. To say that we are changed by living in the pages of scripture is, rather, to suggest that if you and I open our lives to the hope and the demand of the gospel as they are found in scripture, then God will use what we find there to make us want to be better than we know how to be. We will be changed.

## My Life with the Bible

The best way I know to tell you what I mean about how a Bible heard honestly and taken seriously will be used by God's Spirit to change our lives is to leave the door to my life propped open just wide enough for you to see a little slice of my own journey with the sacred scriptures.

Early in my life as a Christian, I embraced the opinion, which was prevalent all around me, that God's call to ministry and the church's ordination to serve were only for men. That was the prevailing, and, as far as I knew, unanimous conviction of all my acquaintances and fellow parishioners. As far as I knew, that was the only "biblical" posture to assume.

When Marcia, Joshua, and I moved to seminary, (there was no Maria back then!), we were invited to assume the pastorate of a wonderful church. I was working at the time as an all-night janitor in Raleigh and going to school in the days (to sleep!) so we really needed a church! But I turned down that wonderful opportunity because it was a church that ordained persons without regard for gender that was, in my fiercely ardent opinion, unbiblical.

I knew how to use the Bible to defend my position, too! I could pick and choose endorsing verses from Corinthians and Timothy and Peter quicker than you could say "old wine skins." But then, slowly and painfully, my old wine skins of opinion began to stretch and creak and bulge at the seams. Under the patient, Christlike scholarship and spirit of folks like John W. Carlton and Randall Lolley, I began, ever so slowly, to wonder if maybe I ought to try hearing the Bible honestly instead of hearing the Bible selectively. I began to wonder if I ought to try taking the Bible seriously instead of claiming to take the Bible literally.

Now this did not all happen in a day. I resisted. I struggled. I closed my eyes to new light. I covered my ears to new truth. I got angry. I held to my old wine skins for all I was worth.

But somehow, by the grace of God, I slowly, painfully began to unlearn the sad art of using the Bible. I slowly, painfully began to take the Bible seriously, which is far more dangerous than taking the Bible literally. I came to understand that the Bible is not a loosely connected set of facts and sayings from which I could pick and choose to suit my taste.

I came to understand that the Bible, the whole Bible, every verse and idea in the Bible must be interpreted against the measure of the supreme revelation of God, Jesus the Christ our Lord. Thus, for me, while the question "Is it biblical?" remained enormously important, the ultimate question became "Is it true to the Spirit of Christ?"

Before, I had trotted out my own comfortable convictions escorted by scripture references that "proved my point," and declared my positions "biblical." Subjecting my "biblical" opinions to the Spirit of Jesus Christ put a great strain on some of my old wine skins, one of which was my "biblical" posture concerning whom God could and could not call to ministry.

As I began to interpret the whole Bible in the light of the life of Jesus Christ, I slowly, painfully came to see that my exclusion of persons from ministry on the basis of their gender simply could not be squared with the spirit of Christ our Lord. I began to acknowledge that most of my "ammunition" against inclusive ministry was written in particular situations to address specific local issues. The old wine skins were straining at the seams and about to burst beneath the weight of new wine and new light, but I wouldn't tell anybody. (Lots of us know better than we act. We believe better than we let on because we feel guilty about moving beyond the traditions and opinions of our past. We have to learn to bless the best of our origins with one hand and grasp the most challenging of our discoveries with the other. But that's grist for another mill and stuff for another sermon!)

Anyway, one day I was reading in Acts 15 about the great debate over whether uncircumcised Gentiles could be saved. I was reading along when I came to Peter's response to all this fussing. The essence of Peter's statement was, "Folks, what we are debating is a moot point. We're arguing over whether or not God can save uncircumcised Gentiles, but I've already been out on the mission field and I've seen them come to salvation and receive the Holy Spirit. God is already doing that which we are debating whether or not God can do! What are we going to do, correct God?"

As I read that passage from Acts 15, the words of scripture became more new wine than those old skins of opinion could accommodate. I finally had to set aside my gender exclusive view of ministry. I knew in my heart that God had always called both God's sons and daughters to minister and serve. I had been debating something that God had already always done. What was I going to do, correct God for calling and using daughters as well as sons? I had to change, and I did. I did not have to change to accommodate culture or feminist theology or modern America; none of that had anything to do with my "internal revolution." I had to change because of the new truth I discovered when I heard the Bible honestly, took the Bible seriously, and interpreted the Bible in the light of the life of Jesus Christ our Lord.

Change, for me, was not easy. (Change seldom is!) To tell the truth, it was a little painful. (Change often is!) What else was I going to do, however, except to be dishonest about what God's Spirit had taught me from the sacred scriptures?

The fact is, when you finally choose to just hear the Bible honestly and take the Bible seriously, you begin to grow. When you begin to "grow in grace, and in the knowledge of our Lord and Savior Jesus Christ," then you will inevitably have to find some new wine skins that can accommodate the new wine that you have found in the words of sacred scripture.

## Conclusion

An open Bible, heard honestly and taken seriously, will be used by the Spirit of God to change us. I guess that's why it is so difficult for us to hear the Bible honestly, take the Bible seriously, and interpret scripture in the light of the life of Jesus the Christ our Savior and Lord. We know that if we ever come to the Bible in that kind of openness, we will, at some point or another, have to change. I can tell you, however, out of the crucible of my own experience, that the pain of change is weightless alongside the freedom and joy that we experience as we "grow up into Christ Jesus."

John Carlton, in *The World in His Heart*, wrote about a preacher who, when asked, "How long does it take to prepare a sermon?" answered, "All my life up to now."[3] This is one of those sermons that has taken me "all of my life up to now." It has taken me all of my life up to now to come to the place that I can hear the Bible honestly and take the Bible seriously. For years my Bible was fenced in by the impertinent barricades of shrill theories of inerrancy and wooden claims of literalism. It has taken me all of my life up to now to set aside such irrelevance and just come to an open Bible with an open heart, seeking, as best I can, to hear the scripture honestly and take the scripture seriously.

I need to warn you, though . . . If you decide to come to the Bible that way, your life will be changed. Not all at once, mind you. But little by little, for as long as you live, new wine will keep bursting old skins.

As a matter of fact, if you decide to hear the Bible honestly and take the Bible seriously, you might want to drop by the bookstore and have them engrave the word "caution" right below "Holy Bible." After all, God does intend for the words of scripture to change our lives into the image of Christ. After all, when you hear it honestly and take it seriously, the Bible does perfectly what God intended for the Bible to do.

> Live in the pages of this book, and it will cause you to be changed.
> Live in the pages of this book, and it will cause you to feel the razor edge of the moral demand of the Christian Gospel.
> Live in the pages of this book, and it will cause you to feel the vast distance between the sky of your intentions and the earth of your performance.
> Live in the pages of this book, and it cause you to empty your pockets for someone else's children.[4]

Wow! Caution! Amen.

## Notes

[1]From a classroom lecture by Professor Ben Philbeck at Southeastern Baptist Theological Seminary; Autumn 1980, Wake Forest, North Carolina.

[2]From Professor Fred Craddock's 1987 Mullins Lectures (audio tape), Southern Baptist Theological Seminary, Louisville, Kentucky.

[3]John W. Carlton, *The World In His Heart*, (Nashville: Broadman Press, 1985) 96.

[4]Craddock.

# The Bible and the Formation of Our Lives

## *Fisher Humphreys*

> How can young people keep their
>     way pure?
> By guarding it according to
>     your word.
> With my whole heart I seek you;
>     do not let me stray from your
>         commandments.
> I treasure your word in my heart,
>     so that I may not sin against
>         you.
> Blessed are you, O Lord;
>     teach me your statutes.
> With my lips I declare
>     all the ordinances of your
>         mouth.
> I delight in the way of your
>         decrees
>     as much as in all riches.
> I will meditate on your precepts,
>     and fix my eyes on your ways.
> I will delight in your statutes;
>     I will not forget your word.
>                 (Psalm 119:9-16)

But be doers of the word, and not merely hearers who deceive
themselves. For if any are hearers of the word and not doers,
they are like those who look at themselves in a mirror; for they
look at themselves and, on going away, immediately forget
what they were like. But those who look into the perfect law,
the law of liberty, and persevere, being not hearers who forget
but doers who act—they will be blessed in their doing. (Jas
1:22-25)

Our wonderful God is a God of grace, a giver rather than a taker.
God's purpose in creating the universe was to form a community of
people to be God's own, people who freely accept God as their God,

receive God's love into their lives, and learn to love God with all their hearts and to love their neighbors as themselves.

Too carry out this purpose, God has provided human beings with a revelation of the divine nature, character, actions, and purposes. The most important medium of God's self-revelation is Jesus Christ, who is the visible image of the invisible God, but God's self-revelation was given through other media as well. For example, God was revealed through mighty acts in history such as the Exodus, the return of Israel from the exile, and the resurrection of Christ. God also was revealed through the religious experiences of persons such as Abraham, Moses, Elijah, Isaiah, Paul, and John. Finally, across many centuries God's self-revelation was written down by prophets and apostles in the collection of books that we call the Bible.

Thus the Bible is one factor in the self-revelation of our wonderful, gracious God. It is a gift to us from God, a means by which we may know God personally and gain an understanding of God's work in the world and in our lives. The Bible is the written Word of God to the people of God.

For this reason, the Bible also is the Holy Book of the church. The church has copied, translated, published, studied, preached, taught, and loved the Bible because the church has believed that it is God's Word to the church.

As the Holy Scriptures of the church, the Bible is a formative factor in the lives of practicing Christians. As we all know, many influences come to bear upon the lives of Christians; we are influenced by the music we hear, the people we meet, the books we read, the experiences we have, and the work we do. As participants in the life of the church, we are influenced by the Bible. More precisely, God uses the Bible to shape and form the lives of Christians.

I want to attempt to answer two questions about the Bible. The first is this: "How does the Bible form our lives?" The second is this: "How can we use the Bible in such a way as to open our lives to its formative power?"

## The Bible as Window and Mirror

How does God use the Bible to form our lives? A valuable distinction for interpreting literature is the one that exists between window-writing and mirror-writing. Window-writing is writing that we look through, to see beyond ourselves and our world to something transcendent. Mirror-writing is writing that we look into, to see a reflection of ourselves and our world so that we can understand them better.

The Bible forms our lives by being both window-writing and mirror-writing in five ways. First, the Bible, as a window, provides us with a worldview. To have one's life formed by the Bible and by the community of faith for whom the Bible is Holy Scripture is to be given a worldview.

Although a worldview may seem to be a theoretical and impractical matter, that is not the case at all. A worldview, a cosmic map, is very real in the consciousness of a people. Indeed, worldviews are found in all communities of people, which suggests that a worldview is an indispensable component in the life of a community.

The worldview of the Bible may be expressed in several ways. For example, it may be understood as a kind of astronomy and geography; that is, it tells us that—above the world we know through our senses—exists an eternal and perfect world called heaven, the home of God, and—beneath the world we experience—exists another world, the world of the damned.

The biblical worldview is also presented very much like a history of the world. It tells us that in the beginning God created a perfect world and an innocent couple, our first parents. Our parents were seduced by a devious tempter and fell from their innocent and blessed state into a state of sin, suffering, and death. Then God graciously intervened to reclaim sinners through Jesus Christ. Finally, at some time in the future, God will act once again to complete the work of redemption and to transform the entire created order into the kingdom of God, a kingdom of justice and peace that will last forever.

The Bible presents its worldview indirectly. The biblical worldview is found between the lines of the Bible rather than on the lines; it is in the background rather than in the foreground.

Nevertheless, the Bible is effective in communicating its worldview to the Christian community. Although the biblical worldview is an enormously sophisticated moral and spiritual vision, the Bible communicates it so successfully that even young children who are brought up in the church manage to internalize it. Many persons who learn this worldview continue to hold it throughout their lives.

As a rule, Christians receive and hold this worldview intuitively and affectively rather than consciously. Ordinarily we do not think about the biblical worldview; rather, we use it to ponder the other things that we learn about ourselves and our world. This worldview provides us with categories for interpreting all of our experiences. These categories exist as presuppositions in the consciousness of the community of faith that is formed by the Bible.

What does the biblical worldview tell us? It tells us that there is a purpose behind our universe; that our world is not the way it was intended to be; that we are entitled to hope for a future when things will be as they should be; that the great Mystery of the world is to be trusted rather than feared; that idols are to be repudiated. There is nothing impractical about being formed by the biblical worldview.

Second, the Bible, as a window, helps us to see and experience God. To be formed by the Bible and the community of faith for whom the Bible is Holy Scripture is to be engaged by God.

There are many kinds of experiences of God. The most familiar to most American Christians is conversion, but there are also experiences of God in prayer, the practice of the presence of God, the encounter with God in the faces of the poor and the suffering, the meeting with God in corporate worship generally and in the Lord's Supper in particular, and others.

Scripture is a catalyst for these and other experiences of God. Sometimes it contributes directly to our experience of God, as we meditate on a that text. More frequently it contributes indirectly. For example, David Kelsey has pointed out that scripture has the power to render an agent—that is, to make God and Jesus come alive for us. By making God real to us, scripture acts as a catalyst for our experience of God. Also, scripture records the stories of religious experiences, such as Moses at the bush, Elijah in the cave, Isaiah in the temple, Paul caught up into a third heaven, and John on the island. These stories foster religious experiences for Christians today.

Third, as a mirror, scripture provides us with practical guidance for living. To be formed by the Bible, and by the community of faith for whom the Bible is Holy Scripture, is to be furnished with practical guidance for life.

People have a deep need for practical guidance. Unlike God's other creatures, human beings are not equipped at birth to know how they ought to live. The popularity of guidance columns in newspapers indicates that people feel a need for practical guidance in their lives.

The Bible provides practical guidance in several formats. There are laws such as the Ten Commandments, stories of people who are examples of how to live and of how not to live, and lists of virtues such as we find in Colossians 3:12 (TEV): "You are the people of God; he loved you and chose you for his own. So then, you must clothe yourselves with compassion, kindness, humility, gentleness, and patience."

There also is the wisdom tradition such as we find in Proverbs. "Wisdom" may be defined as a mastery of life and its difficulties, and guidance into that mastery is provided in the epigrams of Proverbs. "Be generous, and you will be prosperous." "Thoughtless words can wound as deeply as any sword." "Smart people keep quiet about what they know, but stupid people advertise their ignorance." "Work and you will earn a living; if you sit around talking you will be poor." "A gentle answer quiets anger, but a harsh one stirs it up." "If you want people to like you, forgive them when they wrong you." "It is better to meet a mother bear robbed of her cubs than to meet some fool busy with a stupid project." "Being cheerful keeps you healthy. It is slow death to be gloomy all the time." "Enthusiasm without knowledge is not good." "When you give to the poor, it is like lending to the Lord, and the Lord will pay you back" (Prov 11:25, 12:18, 12:23, 14:23, 15:1, 17:9, 17:12, 17:17, 17:22, 19:2, 19:17, TEV).

As we attempt to live our lives by the guidelines that the Bible provides, we find that the worldview and the experiences of God that the Bible gives us are confirmed. As Jesus said, when we will to do God's will, we know the truth of the teaching (John 7:17).

Fourth, as a mirror, scripture incorporates us into the church. To be formed by the Bible is to become a participant in the community of faith for whom the Bible is Holy Scripture.

The Bible knows nothing of private religion. From the beginning, God has been bringing people together into a community. In the Hebrew scriptures they were the descendants of Abraham; in the New Testament they are those who respond in faith to the gospel of Jesus Christ.

For Christians, the biblical stories of the Hebrew people and of the first Christians are not only ancient history, as, for example, the stories of the Roman emperors are. Rather, the stories of God's people in the Bible are, in an important sense, our own story. These characters are our spiritual ancestors. Their survival is indispensable to our existence as a community of faith. Like Ruth the Moabitess, we Christians say that we have traveled where they have traveled and lodged where they have lodged; their people are our people, and their God, our God (Ruth 1:16).

It has been said that the point of literature is to seduce us to live. Similarly, the purpose of Holy Scripture is to seduce us to live in the community whose story is told in scripture.

Finally, as both a window and a mirror, scripture reveals to us our true identity and destiny. To be formed by the Bible and the community of faith for whom the Bible is Holy Scripture is to learn the meaning of our lives.

Paul Tillich has pointed out that in different ages the church has understood salvation in different ways. For example, the fathers of the early church felt keenly their own mortality, so they emphasized salvation as the bestowal of immortality, and the reformers in the sixteenth century were very sensitive to their own guilt, so they stressed salvation as forgiveness or justification. Today we feel deeply the absurdity and meaninglessness of life, so we emphasize that salvation provides the meaning for our existence.

The meaning we seek in life is both simple and a mystery. We long for that which will help us to simplify our lives. We understand the truth of Ecclesiastes (7:29, TEV): "God made us plain and simple, but we have made ourselves very complicated." The meaning of our lives is also a mystery, however, and we know that in some sense it always will remain a mystery. Life is not a puzzle to be solved. As Andrew Louth has written, "We are not concerned with a technique for solving problems but with an art for discerning mystery."

Every day we reach for the Mystery that is God. In our quests for happiness, freedom, knowledge, and love, what we are seeking is the wonderful and mysterious God who is joy, freedom, truth, and love and who generously shares these with us. The Bible shapes our lives by confirming for us that in these self-transcending activities we are in touch with our true identity and our true destiny, and by assuring us that the God to whom we are reaching out in all these ways is a God who knows us and loves us and accepts us and finally delivers us, so that in the end, all will be well.

## Opening Our Lives to the Power of the Bible

We turn now to our second question: How can we use the Bible in such a way that it will exert maximal influence upon our lives? We want to open ourselves to all that God wants to do in our lives by Holy Scripture—What should we do?

Perhaps we can best begin by saying that for most of the church's history, the principal use of the Bible has been corporate rather than private. The Bible has been read aloud in gatherings of the community of faith more frequently than it has been studied privately by individuals. Today, however, we can do both. We should welcome the opportunities for using the Bible privately, but it is very important for the church not to discontinue its ancient practice of reading and thinking about the Bible as a community.

There are several ways we can use the Bible, both corporately and privately. The most obvious use of the Bible is to study it. This is a necessary practice for two reasons. First, the Bible is about the most profound subjects: life, death, love, suffering, God, human destiny. A superficial reading of the Bible cannot do justice to the profound themes about which the Bible speaks. Second, the Bible is an ancient book, written long ago in a world very different from our own, in languages most of us do not know. We study the Bible in order to bridge the gap between that world and ours.

Study is not the only use we can make of the Bible. We can read it. We can read it rapidly as we would any other book in order to catch a glimpse of the larger picture of the Bible, a picture we tend to miss when we study small parts of the Bible intensively. For example, it might take us several weeks to study the book of Philippians, but we can read that book in five or ten minutes. Both procedures are worthwhile. Modern translations are especially helpful when we are reading the Bible.

A third use of the Bible is to hear it. Most Christians throughout the history of the church have received the Bible by hearing it read aloud when they have met for worship. That is why James insisted that we are to be doers of the Word and not *hearers* only (Jas 1:22). We today can hear the Word as the church did in James's day. We can read it aloud in our church services, or we can read it aloud in private, thus receiving the Bible by both our eyes and our ears. We can also listen to it being read aloud by other people on audio and video tapes.

A fourth use of the Bible is to memorize it. Memorization is not as important a part of education today as it was in the past, but it is a practice that we should not surrender altogether. Several programs have been developed for guiding people into memorizing scripture. For many Christians, the best practice is to read until coming across a passage that speaks very deeply. If you find yourself returning to it, you may want to commit it to memory.

A fifth use of the Bible is to sing it. We often do this in church without realizing it; many of our hymns are paraphrases of biblical passages. We also can sing the Bible to ourselves privately. For example, a delightful way to begin the day is to sing quietly to yourself

Psalm 118:24: "This is the day that the Lord hath made; we will rejoice and be glad in it."

A sixth use of the Bible is to take it like medicine. Charles Allen proposed this in his book, *God's Psychiatry*. When Allen was pastor of the First Methodist Church of Atlanta, a successful businessman came to him and asked for help. He said that his work was going well, his family was well, his health was good, but that he was nevertheless dissatisfied with his life. Allen took a piece of notepaper, wrote something on it, folded it, gave it to the man, and said, "Here is my prescription." The man found that Allen had prescribed that he read the twenty-third psalm slowly and deliberately when he first awoke, after each meal, and just before going to sleep, each day for a week. The man objected, but Allen insisted, so the man agreed to try it. A week later he returned and told Allen that the prescription had done the job. Allen said in his book that he had never known it to fail. By reading a passage from the Bible several times during the day, we allow its message to be with us all through the day, and we also have it on our minds as we fall asleep at night.

A seventh use of the Bible is to pray it. The conventional devotional practice is to read the Bible for a few minutes and then to pray for a few minutes. This is a very fine practice. One can also read a verse, pray to God in response to it, then read a little more, and pray in response to it. Consider, for example, the twenty-third psalm. We read, "The Lord is my shepherd." We pause and pray, thanking God for being our shepherd and for calling us to be his sheep. Then we read, "I shall not want." We then pray again, asking God to provide the current needs of which we are aware. Praying the scripture is not a widespread practice, but it is quickly learned and is very helpful, especially at those times when we find it difficult to know what to say in our prayers.

Finally, we can meditate upon the scriptures. This means selecting a very brief passage and repeating it over and over in our minds for several minutes. Meditation is an ancient Christian practice. We can see this, for example, by reading Psalm 119, which contains several references to meditation on God's Word. Unfortunately, for many years we have neglected meditation in the Christian churches; consequently, many Christians have come to associate it with non-Christian religions. We can retrieve this practice for the church today, however, as indeed some Christians are doing. Meditation upon the scripture is simply another way of opening our lives to the influence that God can exert upon us through the inspired writings.

For those of us who want to open ourselves to all that God wants to do in our lives through the Bible there is the word that we heard earlier in James: Be ye doers of the Word and not hearers only. As we attempt to live the life to which we are called by God in scripture, we find that the message of the Bible is authenticated for us. As James said, the person who lives by the Word of God is the one who is blessed by God.

Let us learn to say with the psalmist, "I delight in following your commands more than in having great wealth" (Ps 119:14, TEV).

# A Love Letter from God

## *Robert B. Setzer, Jr.*

Now you have observed my teaching, my conduct, my aim in life, my faith, my patience, my love, my steadfastness, my persecutions and suffering the things that happened to me in Antioch, Iconium, and Lystra. What persecutions I endured! Yet the Lord rescued me from all of them. Indeed, all who want to live a godly life in Christ Jesus will be persecuted. But wicked people and impostors will go from bad to worse, deceiving others and being deceived. But as for you, continue in what you have learned and firmly believed, knowing from whom you learned it, and how from childhood you have known the sacred writings that are able to instruct you for salvation through faith in Christ Jesus. All scripture is inspired by God and is useful for teaching, for reproof, for correction, and for training in righteousness, so that everyone who belongs to God may be proficient, equipped for every good work. (2 Tim 3:10-17)

Years ago, a clergyman took a seat in a dining car of a train traveling along the Hudson River. Opposite him sat a passenger who prided himself on being a card carrying atheist. When this gentleman noticed the minister's clerical collar, his pulse quickened in anticipation of a feisty philosophical fight.

After a few pleasantries were exchanged and lunch was served, the atheist mounted his attack: "I see you're a minister."

"Yes," said the clergyman, "I am a minister of the gospel."

"And I suppose you believe the Bible," the gentleman added, a hint of contempt creeping into his voice.

"Well, yes, I believe God speaks to us through the scripture," the minister answered.

"Well *I* certainly don't," the man shot back. "The Bible is too full of holes for any thinking person to take it seriously." Whereupon, he launched into a withering attack on Holy Scripture.

The minister listened patiently as the gentleman cited a number of supposed contradictions and critical problems within the Bible. While the atheist continued his tirade, the minister simply nodded in acknowledgement and went on eating his dinner. He happened to be dining on Hudson shad, a tasty fish but one noted for its bony structure.

"So tell me," said the atheist, not willing to let the matter drop. "how can you possibly take the Bible seriously, when it is so riddled with problems?"

The clergyman paused to wipe his mouth. "Well, sir, for me, reading the Bible is a lot like dining on this delicious shad. When I come to the bones, I just put them to the side of the plate and go on enjoying my lunch. I leave the bones for some fool to choke on."[1]

## The One to Whom the Bible Points

Many people know just enough about the critical problems raised by serious Bible study to be dangerous. Perhaps they learned in a college Bible course that no serious Old Testament scholar today attributes the first five books of the Old Testament to Moses, at least not in their present form. Along with this, they picked up just enough other tidbits of modern biblical scholarship to recognize that an informed reading of the Bible is not always a simple matter. Such persons know the bones likely to choke modern readers of the Bible, but they have not learned to extract the bones in order to get to the meat of the matter.

Tragically, the higher one ascends on the socioeconomic ladder, the more likely one is to leave the Bible behind. Many have garnered just enough education and sophistication to grow suspect of the Bible. They no longer turn to it for spiritual sustenance. Instead, the Bible is reduced to a family heirloom full of sentimental meaning but devoid of life. It claims a space on the shelf but not in the heart.

Certainly within Baptist ranks, we have compounded the situation in recent years by endless, academic arguments about biblical inspiration. I'll not bore you with the particulars of this debate, except to note that the Southern Baptist Convention has largely self-destructed over something never even addressed in scripture—namely, various *theories* of biblical inspiration. Here in 2 Timothy 3, as throughout Holy Scripture, the reality of the Bible's inspiration is never analyzed or argued about. It is simply affirmed: "All scripture is *inspired* by God" (v. 16).

Yet, it is important to understand that when Paul spoke of the scriptures being "inspired" by God, he was not suggesting that scripture is "inspired" in the same way we might use the term of Shakespeare's sonnets. He meant to make a unique claim for Holy Writ. To translate literally, he was saying that the scriptures are "God-breathed." As God breathed "the breath of life" into Adam's nostrils (Gen 2:7), so God's Spirit led and animated the process by which the Bible was born.

To be sure, the world is full of literature that is inspiring in the usual sense of the word. The Koran, the Baghavad Gita, the Talmud, and Gibran's *The Prophet* all have much to commend them. The Christian claim for the Bible, however, is not that it merely inspires or enlightens, but that it has the power to introduce us to the personal Lord who stands behind its pages. As Paul stated it, "the sacred writings . . . are able to instruct you for salvation through faith in Christ Jesus" (2 Tim 3:15).

According to an old legend, a man became lost in his travels and wandered into a bed of quicksand. Confucius saw the man's predicament and said, "It is evident that men should stay away from places like this." Next, Buddha observed the situation and said, "Let this man's plight be a lesson to those who would not repeat his folly." Then Mohammed came by and said to the sinking man, "Alas, it is the will of God." Finally, Jesus appeared. "Take my hand, brother," said the master, "and let me pull you out."

The world has no shortage of good, inspirational literature, but the Bible alone tells the tale of God's saving act in Jesus Christ . Thus for the Church the Bible can never merely be *a* book, but must ever remain *the* Book. The self-help shelves at the local book store, are loaded with best-selling tips on how to be healthy, wealthy, and wise. But the Bible alone tells us that we don't have to keep trying so hard to "make it," because at the cross of Jesus Christ, God has already gone the ultimate distance to claim us as his own.

Many good and noble truths may be gleaned from wide and varied reading, but only in the Bible do we encounter the truth that sets us free from bondage to sin and death. That is why when believers grow weary of cotton candy and are looking for meat for their souls, it is to the pages of Holy Writ that they turn. For here, and here only, are found the words and works of Jesus, which when breathed upon by the Holy Spirit, become the bread of eternal life.

## The Ones from Whom We Learned the Bible

Thus, on the one hand, the Bible's uniqueness resides in the one *to whom* it points. In commending scripture to Timothy, however, Paul also called on him to remember *from whom* he learned it: "As for you, continue in what you have learned and firmly believed, knowing *from whom* you learned it, and how from childhood you have known the sacred writings" (2 Tim 3:14-15). The reference here is no doubt to Paul, but also to Eunice and Lois, Timothy's mother and grandmother, who were also formative influences in his life (2 Tim. 1:5).

Certainly the caliber of persons from whom I've learned the scriptures has been a pivotal factor in my coming to treasure the Bible. One often hears the cynic's charge that the Church is full of hypocrites. In fairness, I would have to add that while the church no doubt has it share of scoundrels, the finest people I have ever known have been people of the Book.

I think of one of our members who even now is standing by valiantly at the bedside of a dying loved one. Recently, he said to me, "Preacher, I'm sorry I've haven't been able to carry my share down at the church lately, but I've had my hands full."

I assured him I understood and, knowing he was well-versed in scripture, began to quote 1 Timothy 5:8: "Whoever does not provide for relatives, and especially for family members. . . ." But before I could even finish reciting the verse, he filled in the final words as though picking up his half of a litany: "is worse than an unbeliever."

"Yeah, I've thought about that one a lot lately," he continued. "And I've also thought about the fact that Jesus spent thirty years at home working with his family before he spent three years preaching. I reckon my place is at home right now."

The finest people I've ever known have been folks like that, in whose lives the biblical word has played a formative role. When I think of the persons I most admire, it is men and women whose spiritual stature stands as a silent testimony to the power of Holy Scripture to grow a soul.

But Paul's reference to those from whom you learned the scriptures (2 Tim 3:14) not only reminds us of great women and men we have known who loved the Book. It is also a reminder that scripture is not to be approached in isolation, but within a community of learners.

A lot of bizarre and damaging theology has resulted from individuals approaching the Bible as though it were a religious Rorschach test in which the isolated self is free to see whatever he or she chooses. We all come at the Bible with our own particular biases and neuroses intact; these limit what we can see when we look with our eyes only. That's why an opportunity to engage the Bible in small group study—be that in Sunday School, a home Bible Study, or whatever—is essential to the growth of Christian character. Only in the give and take of discussion and dialogue can our own view of scripture and life be challenged and refined by the perspective of others.

One of the Church Fathers told of a monk who secluded himself, eating only one meal a week, trying to discern the meaning of a certain passage of scripture. Yet whenever he asked God to reveal the meaning of the text that troubled him, the heavens fell silent. At last, the monk grew exasperated and said, "Here I have fasted all this time, and it has profited me nothing. I think I shall go and ask my brother."

Just as he shut the door on his way out of the place where he had been cloistered, the angel of the Lord appeared to him and said, "The seventy weeks of your fast have not brought you near to God; but now that you are humbled and going to your brother, I have been sent to show you the meaning of the text." After revealing the text's meaning, the angel departed.[2]

The humility required to study the Bible within a community of learners extends not only to our fellow church members, but also to the community of scholars who make it their life's work to help us better understand the biblical witness. Precisely because the Bible is a particular story drawn from a particular time and place, it must never be severed from its original context. The Bible is not composed of free-floating philosophical wisdom, but of concrete events tied to history and life. The better we understand the original biblical situation, the greater the likelihood we will not distort the Bible's meaning when trying to apply its message to our lives today.

It is my hope that local Baptist churches will ever be places where the best of biblical scholarship is joined to a deeply personal faith, where mind and heart are united in a common quest for spiritual truth. So many of the bones people choke on when trying to read the Bible can be put to the side of the plate, with help drawn from the community of scholars.

I was greatly relieved to learn in my college biblical studies that the creation story in Genesis should be read not as science, but as a poetic description of God's purpose in calling forth the miracle of life. That meant I could read Richard Leaky, Carl Sagan, Stephen Hawking, and other contemporary scientists with an open mind, instead of recoiling from their writings in fear and apprehension.

Since coming to value biblical scholarship, my own approach to Bible reading and study is essentially a two-fold process. On the one hand, I try to familiarize myself with the comments of ancient and modern commentators about a given passage. I consider it the height of arrogance to ignore twenty centuries of Christian reflection when approaching the scriptures. Often what at first glance might appear to be a bone keeping me from the meat of the Word can be put to the side of the plate with a bit of insight or understanding drawn from a brother or sister in the faith.

Having listened to the voices of others, I then listen for a single voice within Holy Writ. I sometimes find that when poring over these ancient pages, a certain Nazarene comes calling from another place and time. In his presence, a challenge I first read as directed to others suddenly rings true within me. A certain word or phrase my mind had passed over a thousand times before snags my attention as though I heard my name called in a crowded room. The story of Sarah, David, Mary, or John draws me into its plot, and I discover new dimensions of myself when I merely intended to study others. In a thousand ways besides, this holy book works its magic, because its author is a living Lord who yet meets those who are his within these sacred pages.

# Conclusion

When all is said and done, Holy Scripture is not a treasure-trove of inspirational readings, however grand and exalted. It is better understood and cherished, as a love letter from God. Most of us can remember the excitement and the joy that bubbled forth when, away at war or at college or a thousand points between, a letter from our beloved arrived. We pored over that letter again and again, trying to wring every drop of meaning from its words in an effort to draw our loved one near.

In an infinitely greater way, the Bible is God's love letter to the world—and not merely because it bears witness to a love of cosmic proportions that led the Savior to die on Golgotha's dark hill. It is also because the author of this book is not merely represented by these words, but is present within them as a sea gull rides the wind.

That is why an open mind before an open Bible must ever characterize those who would grow in the grace and knowledge of the Master. For in and through these murmurings of love, warmed by a breath divine, the very life of God comes to seek and transform our own.

# Prayer

Gracious God, who has gone the limit to save us in our Lord Jesus Christ, we give you thanks for the power of Holy Scripture to sustain us in the pilgrimage of faith. Forgive us all the ways we neglect and disregard your Word, and help us recognize and value it anew within this community of faith as the letter of love it is. Through Jesus Christ our Lord we pray. Amen.

## Notes

[1]*Parables, Etc.*, 5/12 (Saratoga CA: Saratoga Press, 1986) 5.
[2]Roberta C. Bondi, *To Love as God Loves.* (Philadelphia: Fortress, 1987) 105.

# The Best Book of All

## *Karen E. Smith*

Oh, how I love your law!
    It is my meditation all day long.
Your commandment makes me
       wiser than my enemies,
    for it is always with me.
I have more understanding than
    all my teachers,
    for your decrees are my
    meditation.
I understand more than the aged,
    for I keep your precepts.
I hold back my feet from every
       evil way,
    in order to keep your word.
I do not turn away from your
       ordinances,
    for you have taught me.
How sweet are your words to
       my taste,
    sweeter than honey to my
    mouth!
Through your precepts I get
       understanding;
    therefore I hate every false way.

Your word is a lamp to my feet
    and a light to my path.
I have sworn an oath and
       confirmed it,
    to observe your righteous
    ordinances.
I am severely afflicted;
    give me life, O Lord, according
    to your word.
Accept my offerings of praise,
    O Lord,
    and teach me your ordinances.
I hold my life in my hand
    continually,

but I do not forget your law.
The wicked have laid a snare
        for me,
    but I do not stray from your
            precepts.
Your decrees are my heritage
        forever;
    they are the joy of my heart.
I incline my heart to perform
            your statues
        forever, to the end. (Ps 119:97-112)

The law of the Lord is perfect,
    reviving the soul;
the decrees of the Lord are sure,
    making wise the simple;
the precepts of the Lord are right,
    rejoicing the heart;
the commandment of the Lord is
        clear,
    enlightening the eyes;
the fear of the Lord is pure,
    enduring forever;
the ordinances of the Lord are
        true
    and righteous altogether.
More to be desired are they than
        gold,
    even much fine gold;
sweeter also than honey,
    and drippings of the
        honeycomb.

Moreover by them is your servant
        warned;
    in keeping them there is great
        reward.
But who can detect their errors?
    Clear me from hidden faults.
Keep back your servant also from
        the insolent;
    do not let them have dominion
        over me.
Then I shall be blameless,
    and innocent of great
        transgression.

> Let the words of my mouth and
> the meditation of my heart
> be acceptable to you,
> O Lord, my rock and my
> redeemer. (Ps 19:7-14)

So if you have been raised with Christ, seek the things that are above, where Christ is, seated at the right hand of God. Set you minds on things that are above, not on things that are on earth, for you have died, and your life is hidden with Christ in God. When Christ who is your life is revealed, then you also will be revealed with him in glory.

Put to death, therefore, whatever in you is earthly: fornication, impurity, passion, evil desire, and greed (which is idolatry). On account of these the wrath of God is coming on those who are disobedient. These are the ways you also once followed, when you were living that life. But now you must get rid of all such things—anger, wrath, malice, slander, and abusive language from your mouth. Do not lie to one another, seeing that you have stripped off the old self with its practices and have clothed yourselves with the new self, which is being renewed in knowledge according to the image of its creator. In that renewal there is no longer Greek and Jew, circumcised and uncircumcised, barbarian, Scythian, slave and free; but Christ is all and in all!

As God's chosen ones, holy and beloved, clothe yourselves with compassion, kindness, humility, meekness, and patience. Bear with one another and, if anyone has a complaint against another, forgive each other; just as the Lord has forgiven you, so you also must forgive. Above all, clothe yourselves with love, which binds everything together in perfect harmony. And let the peace of Christ rule in your hearts, to which indeed you were called in the one body. And be thankful. Let the word of Christ dwell in you richly; teach and admonish one another in all wisdom; and with gratitude in your hearts sing psalms, hymns, and spiritual songs to God. And whatever you do, in word or deed, do everything in the name of the Lord Jesus, giving thanks to God the Father through him. (Col 3:1-17)

In the church in South Georgia where I grew up, every summer for one week, sometimes two, we went to VBS—Vacation Bible School. It wasn't school at all, of course. We were allowed to wear shorts, and we played games. In craft time we learned over the years the endless number of items that can be made from egg cartons and plastic milk jugs! We drank sweet, sweet orange drink and ate our fill of plain butter cookies. It wasn't like school, but there was time for teaching— Bible teaching.

VBS always began each day in the same way. Each morning the teachers and children gathered outside the church. At the appointed time, the doors opened and everyone marched into the sanctuary. At the front of the procession was a child holding a Bible. Once inside, as part of the opening assembly we would say together the pledge to the Bible:

> I pledge allegiance to the Bible God's holy word. I will make it a lamp unto my feet, a light unto my path and I will hide its words in my heart that I might not sin against God.

As the years have passed, I have often thought about the women who willingly gave up their time to come and teach us about God's love. They loved God and believed in Bible teaching. While I give thanks to God for those who taught me to love the Bible, I'm not sure that our early Baptist forbears would have agreed with the idea of saying a pledge to the Bible. They most certainly would have frowned upon the accompanying pledge to the American flag and the Christian flag that was also a part of each VBS assembly! Yet, I feel certain about one thing: Our early Baptist mothers and fathers would have agreed that the psalmist was right when he wrote, "Your Word is a lamp unto my feet and a light unto my path."

The voice of the psalmist was the voice of one who, of course, had known plenty of darkness. He had known the darkness of grief and the darkness of despair. "I am severely afflicted," he wrote. "The wicked have laid a snare for me" (Ps 119:107,110). On another occasion he wrote, "My tears have been my food day and night, while people say to me continually, 'Where is your God?' " (Ps 42:3). He had known what it was to feel trapped in a "desolate pit and a miry bog" (Ps 40:2). The psalmist experienced deep, deep darkness. Yet, he knew that the Word could cast light in dark places, within us as well as outside of us.

This light-casting power may be why none of us spends enough time reading and studying the Word. The Word lightens our path as it enables us to see ourselves more clearly. If we go to the Word of God with an unresolved grudge and knowing that we have not forgiven someone, the Word of God that comes back to lighten our path is this: "Do not let the sun go down on your anger" (Eph 4:26). Even God is "kind to the ungrateful and the wicked" (Luke 6:35).

If we go to the Word of God with a spirit of greed, the Word that comes back to illumine our path is this: "You received without payment; give without payment" (Matt 10:8).

If we go to the Word of God thinking that we have everything under control and really do not need God's help at all, the Word that comes back to illumine our path is this: "Those who are well have no need of a physician, but those who are sick; I come to call not the righteous but sinners" (Mark 2:17).

If we go to the Word of God with a judgmental and critical attitude, the Word of God that comes back to illumine our path is this: "Do not judge, so that you may not be judged. . . . Why do you see the speck in your neighbors eye, but do not notice the log in your own eye?" (Matt 7:1,3).

The Word of God is a lamp to those who are seeking the way forward in truth and sincerity. Of course, that light may not be shed on every dark corner at once. There will always be questions of faith and questions about life—dark questions—for which we cannot seem to find an answer. Why did the doctor not come sooner? Why were we away from home when he became ill? Why were we not allowed a few more years together?

Our darkness is sometimes punctuated by questions that we cannot answer. Some of our questions may not be exposed to the light until the morning breaks bright and fair for us on that eternal day when we are greeted by Divine Love. But I am that if we will turn to the Bible and make it a lamp unto our feet, there will always be enough light to see the next step. Sometimes it is no more than that, but there is always enough light for the moment.

His name was Joe Neal Anderson, and he lived all of his life in Marrowbone, Kentucky. Joe Neal was eighty-five when he learned to read. He had grown up in a large farming family, had worked hard all of his life, and had never had the opportunity to learn to read. When he was eighty-five, listening to the radio one day he heard that there was a new method to teach adults to read. He mentioned it to his fifty-year-old niece, Grace Anderson. She decided that if Uncle Joe Neal wanted to learn, she would try to help him.

Learn he did, though he claimed that at first he thought he could never learn to read. "It just looked solid to me like one big wall, but then I broke into it," he said.[1] When asked what books he liked to read, Joe Neal replied, "Well I may read them all, but the main one is the Bible because it's the leader."[2]

The Word of God, wrote the psalmist, is "more to be desired than gold, even much fine gold; sweeter also than honey, and drippings of the honeycomb" (Ps 19:10). Indeed it is, "the leader"—the best book of all, as it lights our way. The Word will not light our way, though, unless we "hide it in our hearts." The last part of the VBS pledge is perhaps the most important and the most difficult. It is one thing to read the Bible, it is quite another to "let the Word of Christ dwell in you richly" (Col 3:16). It takes almost no effort at all to read a few verses a day and claim to have done our "daily Bible reading" for the day. To meditate upon the Word so that the words of our mouths and the meditations of our hearts will be acceptable to God is another matter.

The early Baptists certainly took seriously the idea of letting the Word dwell within them. At one level, they understood this as hiding the Word of God in their hearts as they pondered its meaning and meditated upon it. Sermons were structured in a way that was intended to help the listeners to remember the text and recall the minister's exposition. I remember reading the diary of one eighteenth-century English Baptist woman who continually referred to passages of scripture that had given her help. Time and time again in her journal she would be pondering some event or problem in life and she would say: "and I thought again of that word . . ." and she would cite a passage of scripture. One had the feeling that, as she lived and worked somehow by the power of the Holy Spirit, the Living Word was shaping and transforming her life as she allowed it to teach her and admonish her. The Word of Christ was dwelling in her richly.

The early Baptists knew what Joe Neal Anderson found out for himself—the Bible is the leader. I am glad that I grew up in a Baptist church in South Georgia and went to Vacation Bible School each summer, for it was there that I learned, too, that the Bible is the best book of all. Let us pray that the Word of Christ will, indeed, dwell in us richly so that "whatever you do in word or deed, do everything in the name of the Lord Jesus" (Col 3:17).

## Notes

[1]Byron Crawford, "A New Chapter, Cumberland County Man finds a world of words at 85," *The Courier Journal* (Louisville KY, 1989).
    [2]Ibid.

# How Baptists Read the New Testament

## William E. Hull

> Beloved, while eagerly preparing to write to you about the salvation
> we share, I find it necessary to write and appeal to you to contend for
> the faith that was once for all entrusted to the saints. (Jude 3)

What ultimately is at stake in belonging to the family of faith called
Baptists?[1] In trying to answer that question, I have remembered again
and again the earliest definition ever taught me of a Baptist church,
an understanding that remains for me, after thirty years in the ministry, the clearest and most consistent self-witness of our denomination
to its deepest identity. It derives primarily from the central article in
our historic confessions, all of which declare Holy Scripture to be the
sole rule of faith and order.[2] Stated in simplest form, the controlling
norm that has always been constitutive of our organized life as
Baptists is the conviction that we exist for no other reason than to be
New Testament churches. Surely we are correct in identifying this
commitment, above all others, as "The Baptist Ideal."

Our determination to establish, enlarge, and extend New Testament churches does not signal a desire to live in the ancient past, to
resist historical change, or to ignore the modern world.[3] Far from
attempting to make time stand still, our concern is to actualize the
apostolic faith in each new age, to transcend the strictures of the
status quo by allowing the unique Christ-event to triumph in our
time. Our ancestors realized that we must look back to the normative
mid-point of holy history for controlling clues to our enduring
responsibilities. Our mandate is determined by God's unique revelation in Jesus Christ, as seen through the pages of the New Testament,
rather than by the weight of tradition, the authority of creeds, or the
pronouncements of councils. In our ecclesiology, not only the individual but the congregation must be reborn; that is, neither a person
nor a church can live by a "succession" mediated through history.
Both must be quickened by an encounter with the eternal Word-made-
flesh who is ever our contemporary through the Holy Spirit.

When we ask what is involved in implementing this Baptist ideal, the answer must be that we first discover the dominant features of New Testament Christianity and then reproduce those same essential characteristics in our churches today. We are not seeking a slavish imitation of outer form but a creative equivalence of inner spirit. When I step back and examine the total sweep of scriptural witness, I find three hallmarks of apostolic faith so prominent that one simply could not imagine a New Testament church without them. I propose that we first define each of these distinctive attributes as they flourished in the first century and then make them the criteria by which to measure the adequacy of our faithfulness as Baptists in the last decade of the twentieth century.

## A Person

Clearly the most conspicuous mark of every New Testament church was its Christ-centeredness. The early Christians sought to cultivate the mind of Christ (Phil 2:5), to follow in the steps of Christ (1 Pet 2:21), and to function as the Body of Christ (1 Cor 12:27). One simple preposition says it best: they were "*in* Christ" (2 Cor 12:2), and Christ was "*in* them" (Col 1:27). Everything followed from this reciprocal relationship: they were crucified "with Christ" (Col 3:1). Listen to Paul exhaust human language in paying tribute to his centrality: "[A]ll things have been created through him and for him. He himself is before all things, and in him all things hold together. He is the head of the body, the church; he is the beginning, the firstborn from the dead, so that he might come to have first place in everything" (Col 1:16-18).

This preeminence of a historical person stood in sharp contrast to the leading options afforded by first century religious life. Judaism offered the Pharisees with their traditionalism, the Sadducees with their elitism, the Essenes with their sectarianism, and the Zealots with their nationalism. Hellenism offered philosophical movements such as neo-Platonism, ethical movements such as Stoicism, and mystical movements such as Gnosticism. Idealogy was rampant; "-isms" were everywhere!

Strangely enough, however, we hear nothing of all this in the New Testament. Instead of analyzing an idea, defending a concept, or pushing a proposition, the writers were forever describing a person: how he lived, what he taught, the issues for which he stood, the spirit in which he served. It would have been natural, almost inevitable, to be drawn into the burning debates of the day. Paul was constantly pressed by the "wise" to interpret Christianity in terms of the popular slogans of his time (1 Cor 1:18-2:15), but he decided instead "to know nothing among you except Jesus Christ, and him crucified" (1 Cor 2:2).

Today, we are again caught in the cross-fire of competing ideologies. Most of the same old alternatives are still with us, such as traditionalism, elitism, sectarianism, nationalism, and even a touch of Gnosticism. The terms used more prominently are "conservatism" and "liberalism," with their extremes of "fundamentalism" and "modernism." Thrown into the debate for good measure are such fighting words as "rationalism," "radicalism" and "relativism"—labels all the more dangerous because so many people have no clear idea of what they mean!

The difference today is not that our world is seething with so much abstract speculation, for such was the situation in the first century as well. Rather, the contract lies in the way that this partisan debate has infiltrated the very heart of our Baptist life. Over and over we are told that we must decide finally for or against some "-ism," whereas the New Testament declares that our only ultimate choice is for or against Jesus Christ. Some of our most vocal modern apostles seem determined to preach their personal views on conservatism or liberalism, whereas Paul said, "We proclaim Jesus Christ as Lord and ourselves as your slaves for Jesus' sake" (2 Cor 4:5). All of a sudden our sins have become ideological. Now we point a finger at those who are guilty of "humanism" or "secularism," whereas in the New Testament sin was relational, a personal rebellion against God, a rejection of his Messiah (Acts 2:36-37).

Studying all of the ideological options and then choosing a personal position is certainly not wrong. The only problem comes when these various alternatives are confused with the Christian faith. We are not saved by a proposition but by a Person. We are not judged by the adequacy of our concepts but by the authenticity of our commitments. Let those who are "wise" enough to analyze abstract theories go off to a seminar room and debate their viewpoints, but let us stand in our pulpits and on our street corners and proclaim, not an impersonal slogan, but an indwelling Savior! Let us give people a Leader, not a label! That is what the New Testament churches did, and that is what our Baptist ideal calls us to do today.

# A Presence

One problem with ideas, however valid, is that they are static and impersonal, whereas a person is active and dynamic. Unlike the finest of propositions, Christ talked back to his disciples, guiding and correcting and encouraging them along each step of "the way" (Acts 9:2). Because he was alive in his risen Spirit, every New Testament church was both a Christocentric community and a Pneumatic community. That is, early Christians were not only the people of a Person but the people of a Presence as well.

This sense of being Spirit-filled and Spirit-led enabled them to avoid a "museum" mentality as time and space increasingly separated their life from the Palestine of A.D. 30. On a tour of New England, I visited the Hawthorne house in Salem, the Paul Revere house in Boston, and the Emerson house in Concord, all of them preserved exactly as furnished when inhabited by greatness. The early Christians never even tried to turn back the clock. They built no shrines in Nazareth or collected any relics in Jerusalem, for their founder was not behind them, buried in the past, but out before them as they crossed every new frontier into the future. They followed not footprints in the sands of time but listened for the footfalls of one who promised, "I am *with you always*, to the end of the age" (Matt 28:20).

Abundant evidence of divine guidance is seen in the sense of spiritual freedom reflected throughout the New Testament. Unlike the Judaizers, who insisted that the faith be subservient to the age-long religious traditions of the Old Testament, the mainstream of the Christian movement soon abandoned the practice of circumcision, the centrality of one Temple in Jerusalem with its sacrificial system, and even the observance of the Sabbath and the annual Jewish festivals. These institutions had been central bulwarks in their inherited faith, explicitly commanded over and over again by scripture. We can be certain that the New Testament would never have made such a radical departure from the Old Testament had not the early Christians felt the clear guidance of the Holy Spirit to do so. No wonder Paul cried in the midst of this revolution, "Where the Spirit of the Lord is, there is *freedom!*" (2 Cor 3:17).

Note that this liberty to innovate did not become a license to reject scripture. When the day of worship was changed from Saturday to Sunday, when infant circumcision was replaced by adult baptism, and when the one centralized Temple was superseded by scattered local congregations, there is no hint that those alterations were made because the former practices were somehow in "error." These and other drastic changes did not come about because the New Testament churches suddenly decided to go on a "liberal" binge, but because they were certain that the Spirit of God was leading them to discover the deeper intention of the Old Testament. Far from compromising the authority of scripture, the apostles rejoiced that they had been privileged to behold its fulfillment (Matt 5:17-18).

Today, in place of celebrating our Spirit-led freedom to discover the deeper meaning of scripture, we often find a cautious conformity to the status quo that stifles such a search. Ignoring the promise of Jesus that the Holy Spirit will guide us into a fuller understanding of truth (John 16:13), some timid voices insist that we halt our pilgrimage at the level of insight reached by our predecessors in 1963, 1925, or even 1833.[4] Baptist history should have taught us that our peculiar destiny as a "free church" denomination is to break the shackles of traditionalism even if it means sailing on uncharted seas or preaching from Virginia jails. Can we ever forget those stirring words of John Robinson to the Pilgrims as they set forth on the "Mayflower" in 1620 to escape the religious tyranny of Europe: "The Lord has more light and truth yet to break forth out of His holy Word."[5]

In the present political climate, it is easy to resist any innovation simply by labeling it as "liberalism." Nor can it be denied that some liberals are quick to follow the latest fad, to embrace newness for its own sake. In the Bible, though, one does not have to be a "liberal" to be an agent of revolutionary change. One has only to be filled with the Spirit of him who cried, "See, I am making all things *new*" (Rev 21:5; cf. Isa 43:19).

Ironically, our caution in daring any great venture may testify that we are being influenced more by the spirit of conservatism in our culture than by the wind of the Spirit that "blows where it wills" (Jn 3:8). Can it be that we have faltered in our missionary task because we have taken our eyes off the pillar of cloud by day and pillar of fire by night that would lead us through the wilderness to conquer a new promised land for God (Exod 13:21-22)? As Stephen saw so clearly, the divine Presence is a restless reality that keeps us on the move toward places we have never been before (Acts 7:2-53.)

# A Passion

In the New Testament, the most daring change that the Spirit of God freed the churches to make was not the abandonment of such key Old Testament realities as Sabbath, circumcision, and Temple. Rather, these practices were superseded as a natural consequence of the freedom that the early Christians felt to move out beyond the bounds of Judaism to every person regardless of race, nationality, or culture. In other words, God allowed them to jettison a great deal of ancient Jewish baggage, not in order to become more "liberal," but to become more open and flexible in winning the world to Christ. This was an overriding desire, that *"every* knee should bow" in homage to Jesus Christ as Lord. Here, then, was their third dominant characteristic: to be not only the people of a Person and of a Presence but also the people of a Passion to share the gospel with every person on earth.

This universal inclusiveness stood in sharp contrast to the narrow exclusiveness of the parent faith. The Book of Acts is essentially a story of how love leaped over barriers that had stood for centuries in order to embrace believers of every background. Ironically, in the crucial period from A.D. 30–70, Judaism was girding itself for a fight to the finish with the very "foreigners" whom Christianity was seeking to save. This comparison implies no superiority on the part of the early disciples, however, as if they were less provincial or prejudiced than their Jewish compatriots. Both the record in Acts and the struggles in the letters of Paul make painfully clear that the apostles became world missionaries almost in spite of themselves. Without intending so drastic a revolution, they were surprised to discover that when they preached Christ two things happened: First, anyone who heard the Gospel felt free to respond because it placed all humanity on equal footing before God. Second, the Holy Spirit had a habit of racing ahead of his servants and authenticating the conversion of Gentiles even before the church was ready to receive them (Acts 10:44-48; 11:15-18).

As the early Christian congregations began to include all manner of converts, dividing the movement into several denominations would have been natural. After all, here were the most diverse groups imaginable trying to live in the most intimate kind of fellowship— Jews and Greeks, slaves and freedmen, barbarians and Scythians. But they did not fragment along earthly lines because Christ was "all, and in all" (Col 3:11). In other words, the earliest Christians set out not only to reconcile the whole world to Christ but to do so "in *one* body" (Eph 2:16), rather than dividing up such an awesome assignment among several splinter groups.

That same task is precisely the challenge of Baptist missions today. The Baptist goal is to share the gospel not with every Southerner, American, Anglo-Saxon, or every conservative, but with every person in *the whole world*. In accepting the missionary mandate of the New Testament, we define our churches as inclusive enough for all of those committed to the lordship of Christ. True to the spirit of the New Testament, we must not pick our preferences and try to win them, leaving the rejects for other denominations. No, *every* church must do *every* thing possible to win *every* person to Christ.

Our attempt to make Christian outreach the presiding passion of Baptist life is being confused by secular efforts to "positionize" us in the religious marketplace. According to this perspective, Baptists are supposed to appeal to the 19% of the American population who view themselves as "evangelical" or to the 47% who view themselves as "conservative," leaving the rest to be serviced by "mainline" denominations that are more "liberal." Baptist thinking has been influenced by a Gallup Poll mentality that is all the more seductive because it congratulates us on being among the largest "evangelical" denominations in a day when "conservatism" is IN. Why worry, the pollsters insinuate, when you're on top with the tide running in your favor?

Why indeed! Because our task is not to outnumber the Methodists but to win the world—a world in which every day there are more lost persons than the day before. God has not raised up Baptists to lead the Gallup Poll sweepstakes but to empty hell of its prospective tenants! The Christ whom we preach did not say, "And I, when I am lifted up from the earth, will draw all people to myself" (cf. John 12:32). The Great Commission did not command, "Go ye into all the South and make disciples of every Anglo-Saxon" (cf. Matt 28:19-20). No great harm lies in letting the pollsters classify us, as long as we refuse to become captive to their categories, as long as we let their results suggest where we may have narrowed the universality of our appeal, and as long as we constantly confound them by breaking out of every cultural mold to carry the gospel into forbidden territory.

Baptists were never meant to be simply one denomination among many in the sense of occupying a narrow spot on the contemporary religious spectrum. Just as the apostolic age knew no denominations in the modern sense, we are called to transcend all such distinctions by determining to be nothing other than a cooperating fellowship of New Testament churches. Our only heritage is that which insists on making every heritage captive to the Word of God. Our validity is not determined by whether we are riding the latest sociological band-wagon, whether we happen to endorse the right candidate for president of the United States, or whether we can capitalize on the ascendancy of the sunbelt in American culture. Rather, our authenticity is confirmed when we demonstrate that what God did for people two thousand years ago in the sending of Jesus Christ God can do yet again in each new time and place.

How shall Baptists read the New Testament? By living ourselves into the reality of apostolic Christianity until its spirit becomes our spirit and its atmosphere pervades our churches. Our task is not to build electronic churches or charismatic churches or renewal churches but *New Testament churches*: grounded in the Person of Christ our Savior, hounded by the restless Presence of his risen Spirit, and bounded by a world whose winning is the overriding Passion of our lives.[6]

## Notes

[1]I sought to probe the same question for an academic community in my commencement address, "Whatever Happened to the Baptist Ideal?" delivered at The Southern Baptist Theological Seminary, Louisville, Kentucky, May 30, 1975.

[2]Baptist confessions of faith began in earnest with the London Confession of 1644, which, in article VII, defined "the Rule of this Knowledge, Faith, and Obedience" as "only the word of God contained in the Canonical Scriptures." The next great testament to Baptist faith was the Second London Confession of 1677 that moved the article on the Bible to Chapter I and began it by affirming that "the Holy Scripture is the only sufficient, certain, and infallible rule of all saving Knowledge, Faith, and Obedience." In the United States, the New Hampshire Confession of 1833 referred to the Bible as "the supreme standard by which all human conduct, creeds, and opinions should be tried," and this language was repeated virtually unchanged in the Southern Baptist confessions of 1925 and 1963. For references, see William L. Lumpkin, *Baptist Confessions of Faith* (Philadelphia: Judson Press, 1959) 158, 248, 393.

[3]On the difficulties and dangers of theological repristination see Robert L. Wilken, *The Myth of Christian Beginnings* (Garden City: Doubleday, 1971). My plea is not that Baptists "idealize" a timeless apostolic age, but that their ideal be the translation of this epoch, in all its historical particularity, into the life of today. In other words, just as we must translate ancient languages (i.e. Greek) into modern languages (i.e. English), so we must translate ancient life (i.e. of apostolic Christianity) into modern life (i.e. of contemporary Christianity). On this hermeneutical

enterprise see my essay, "The Theological Task of Baptists Today," *The Truth That Makes Men Free*, edited by Josef Nordenhaug (Nashville: Broadman, 1966) 445-52.

[4]The dates refer to some of the leading Baptist confessions of faith discussed above in note 2.

[5]Quoted by H. Wheeler Robinson, *The Life and Faith of the Baptists* (London: Kingsgate, 1946) 13.

[6]A version of this sermon was preached as the Convention Sermon to the 133rd session of the Louisiana Baptist Convention meeting in the First Baptist Church, New Orleans, November 11, 1980. Printed in the 1980 *Annual of the Louisiana Baptist Convention* (Alexandria: LBC Executive Board, 1980) 256-60.

# How baptists Read the Bible

## H. Stephen Shoemaker

In Will Campbell's novel, *The Glad River*, the main character, Doops Momber, refuses to get baptized because he can't find a real baptist left to do the baptizing. Throughout the book he is looking for a real baptist.

So are we. Would we know one if we saw one? I begin with the question: Is there a peculiar way baptists read scripture that leads to a distinctively baptist mode of preaching? If so, then it is important to identify it so that we can carry on the living baptist way of being Christian and offer it as a witness to the world and to the ecumenical fellowship of Christians.

Mark number one is signaled in the way I have spelled baptist in the title. Following James McClendon's lead,[1] I now spell baptist with a lower case b. This better represents the character of the believers' church or free church tradition, the way we call baptist. We are a dissenting minority, strong in conviction and modest in voice. We are anti-authoritarian and anti-triumphalist. So we spell our name with a small b, just as we spell church with a small c.

I have compared denominationalism with the story of the blind man and the elephant. One blind man held the elephant around the leg and proclaimed that the elephant was like a tree; one touched the elephant on the trunk and said the elephant was like a great snake; a third touched the side of the elephant and said it was like a wall; the last grabbed hold of its tail and said, No, the elephant is like a rope! They stood and argued all day long.

Each denomination has hold of some part of the elephant. We should hold with deep conviction that the part we hold is truth about Christ. But we should also acknowledge that we are blind—we see through a glass darkly—and that we hold only a part of the truth. That is how we combine fervent conviction with modesty of voice. With such conviction and modesty we baptists joyfully and unashamedly offer what we have to the world.

# The Peculiar Way baptists Read Scripture

Is there a peculiar way we baptists hold and read and interpret scripture? There is and it is peculiar. As Flannery O'Connor paraphrased Jesus:

> You shall know the truth
> And the truth shall make you odd.

Following Abraham and Jesus our vision is, to use the poet Hopkins' words, "counter, original, spare, strange."[2]

The baptist way or baptist vision is made up of at least these characteristics.

(1) As a believers' church we offer baptism only to those who believe and have freely chosen to follow Christ. We would hope the church would be such a place of Christian nurture that, in the words of Horace Bushnell, the children would grow up a Christian and never know themselves as being otherwise, but we also believe for every person conversion, which marks our turning to and following Christ, is prompted by the Holy Spirit. Our children are the first to whom we carry the gospel on mission. But not just one conversion, many. To paraphrase the thought of another: the power of sin is so strong both within us and around us and the gospel of Christ is so demanding and different, it takes a lifetime of conversions to become the new creations God made us to be.[3] Baptism as symbol of the birth of faith, of the first and ongoing conversion into Christ, and of entrance into the church is practiced as believers' baptism in the believers' church.

(2) We are a free church. As a free church we affirm: (a) "soul competency" and "soul freedom."[4] These old phrases affirm that every individual believer is competent under the guidance of the Holy Spirit to open the Bible and interpret it for his or her own life and faith—and if competent must also be free. (b) We stand for "local church autonomy," which says that the local congregation is competent, has all *it* needs, under the guidance of the Holy Spirit, to open the Bible and interpret it for its life and faith—and if competent must also be free from higher ecclesial or civic authorities. (c) As a free church we stand for religious liberty for all people and for the institutional separation of church and state. We have protected freedom of

conscience with our life blood, and the First Amendment to the Constitution of the United States of America has baptist fingerprints all over it.

We have gone to jail and been killed for our zeal to protect the freedom of conscience of all people, even for people whose faith is different, even for those who choose no faith. We stand for *voluntarism* in spiritual matters. A coerced faith is no faith at all.

(3) We are a biblical people with a biblicist tradition. Biblicism is not to be equated with one or another theory of inspiration but is the humble acceptance of biblical authority. Biblicism is to be distinguished from bibliolatry. Biblicism reads and follows an open Bible. Bibliolatry worships a closed one, waves it as a prideful banner or wields it as a weapon. A biblical people live with an open Bible, pledge to follow it with their lives and believe with John Robinson, early Separatist pastor of a group of exiles in Holland, that "God hath yet more light and truth to break forth out of his Holy Word."[5]

(4) We are an evangelical people, but I define us carefully so in three ways.

(a) In the Protestant sense of the word, we are Christo-centric. Christ and his gospel is the center and circumference of our life. We read scripture and live life in light of the central revelation of God in Christ.

(b) In the context of modern evangelicalism we are the kinds of evangelicals who treasure experience over doctrine. (For some other evangelicals, doctrine is primary.) Personal relationship with Christ is the saving, essential thing and more crucial than orthodoxy of doctrine. "Our only creed is the Bible," we say, and we sing:

> My faith has found a resting place not in device nor creed.
> I trust the ever-living one, his wound for me shall bleed.
> I need no other argument, I need no other plea.
> It is enough that Jesus died, and that he died for me.

We have tended to de-emphasize dogma, doctrine, and creeds. In the London Confession of 1677 we borrowed heavily and gratefully from the Westminster Confession and Savoy Confession (early Congregational) not only to voice agreement but to also communicate, in the words of the confession, "that we have no itch to clog religion with new words."[6]

(c) We are a people committed to world evangelization. I prefer this word to evangelism because evangelism tends to concentrate on the one moment of first turning or conversion. Evangelization, however, honors the whole glorious and mysterious process by which a person comes to faith and lives in Christ: the sharing of the gospel, the birth of faith in the hearer, baptism, incorporation in the body of Christ, and the empowerment and equipping of all his saints for mission and ministry.

(5) We are communal-faith people. (This dimension is especially the gift of early anabaptist faith and is more evident in the baptist fellowship around the world today than in the hyper-individualist forms of baptist life in the United States.) Our emphasis on believers' baptism and the local church as the basic unit of Christianity puts an emphasis on the church as community. Our community orientation is careful, though, not to squash the individual and deny freedom of conscience. So there is a unity in diversity and diversity in unity. In democratic self-government the baptist church forges its own common life under God and God's Word, but it also honors the dissent of the individual and minority *within* the church, just as baptists protect the dissent of individuals and minorities in the civic sphere. E. E. Cummings said of the mystery of marriage: "We are so both and oneful." We could say, Cummings—like, of the mystery of community: "We are so many and onesome, so oneful and many."

Some communitarian movements are formed by way of the death of individual freedom. Some communities are destroyed by the individualism of its members. The baptist vision is committed to a strong community that has diversity in its unity because of its respect for the individual grasp of truth and for individual freedom.

(6) We have the ever vigilant perspective of a dissenting minority. We live and read scripture with a "hermeneutics of suspicion" against every form of tyranny: the tyranny of the majority over the minority, the tyranny of the state over its citizens, the tyranny of religious leaders over religious communities, the tyranny of pastors over churches.

"Southern Baptists" have largely lost this perspective. We have become establishmentarian in character rather than having the identity of a dissenting minority. With this establishment-religion posture, we've lost our identification with and advocacy for the minority and marginalized peoples of our world. We've been tempted to become the "moral majority" oppressing minority stances of dissenters. African-American and Third-World baptists and East European and Russian baptists are better witnesses to this dimension of being baptist than we now are. In fact, the best way to become real baptists today is to become world baptists.

These are marks of being baptist, and I am pleased to associate myself with this crowd, even though it seems to be an endangered species and even though our present pretensions and heresies have turned us into a rather strange animal—like Brer Rabbit dressed up like Brer Bear, or Roger Williams preaching in Jerry Falwell's Thomas Road Baptist Church. If Roger would show up he'd say: "This is baptist? This looks more like the bunch who kicked me out of the Massachusetts Bay Colony for *being* a baptist!" I've often thought we should form a non-geographical baptist association called the Roger Williams baptist association and invite to join every church disfellowshiped from a local association or convention and every person denied ordination or commissioning based on differences of biblical interpretation: charismatics, women, divorced people, liberals, snake handlers. Why, this association might even begin to look like the early church!

## The baptist Way of Preaching Scripture

If those are the marks of the baptist way of being Christian and reading scripture, is there a baptist way of preaching that follows? I think so.

(1) In a believers' church, baptist preaching preaches for conversion, for that first turning to Christ and for the ongoing conversion of the believer into a new creation in Christ. It is evangelical preaching in that it calls people to Christ and to personal decision.

(2) In the free church tradition baptist preaching is an act of freedom. We are utterly free under God to seek the truth in scripture wherever it may lead and to seek the truth anywhere in life, unafraid that any truth that is truth will contradict scripture, for God is the God of all truth. Baptist preaching is an act of freedom from any higher human authority, ecclesial or civic.

But baptist preaching is also a modest act. We do not preach as "ruler of the church," to use W. A. Criswell's phrase, or as infallible interpreter of scripture. To quote the apostle Paul: "For we do not proclaim ourselves; we proclaim Jesus Christ as Lord and ourselves as your slaves for Jesus' sake" (2 Cor 4:5). We are not only servants of the Word but also servants of God's people. These words come from 2 Corinthians where Paul was up to his eyeballs in alligators battling the "super-apostles," those traveling missionary preachers who were tyrannizing the faith of the Corinthians. No wonder Paul was careful to say, "I do not mean to imply that we lord it over your faith; rather, we are workers with you for your joy." (2 Cor 1:24). These "super-apostles" pranced into Corinth impressive in appearance, superb of speech; and look what they did to the church. Paul said,

> For you put up with it when someone makes slaves of you, or preys upon you, or takes advantage of you, or puts on airs, or gives you a slap in the face. To my shame, I must say, we were too weak for that. (2 Cor 11:20-21)

So is baptist preaching. Baptist preaching is preaching in weakness, the weakness of the cross, the weakness of our frail earthen vessels, knowing that God's strength is made perfect in weakness, trusting that the transcendent light shines through our cracked clay pots.

Eduard Schweizer, world-acclaimed New Testament scholar and preacher from Zurich, was asked once while spending a term in America, "What do you think of American preaching (including much baptist preaching)?" He said, *"It is too perfect!"* When I recently had a chance to ask him to explain his answer, he said that the American preacher exercises splendid rhetorical skills and gives the impression that once he has preached this sermon he has said all that needs to be said about the text. In contrast, Schweizer said, the preacher should stand bent and waiting with the people reaching for God to speak to us and reveal more to us. Preaching is an act of humble waiting, partial exposition, truth seeking yet more truth. Baptist preaching at its best has this posture of modesty.

If we believe in soul competency, freedom of conscience, then we will not presume to "lord it over" God's people but rather to interpret it as a priest among a congregation of priests.

(3) As people on a biblical tradition we combine intellectual rigor in our study of scripture with evangelical warmth. Thomas McKibbens, baptist preacher, scholar, and historian, has reminded us in his important book, *The Forgotten Heritage: A Lineage of Great Baptist Preaching*,[7] that we come from a great line of preachers who combined head and heart, learning and piety. John Smyth, Thomas Helwys, John Bunyan, William Carey, Andrew Fuller, Richard Furman, H. Wheeler Robinson, John Broadus, on and on, combined hard intellectual work with warm piety that together made salvation's strong and fervent appeal to the world.

John Bunyan pictured the preacher in *Pilgrim's Progress* by way of a picture on the wall of the Interpreter's House:

> It had eyes lift up to Heaven, the best of Books in his hand, the Law of Truth was written upon his lips, the World was behind his back; it stood as if it pleaded with Men.[8]

How much modern critical biblical scholarship does the preacher need? Enough to match his/her general learning in all areas and enough to answer all the questions that the simple reading of scripture raises for him or her. How much critical scholarship does the congregation need? Raymond Brown answers well: enough to match their general level of knowledge in other fields. This is a good rule, for knowledge in these other fields—science, history, geology, literature, and so on—will bring more questions to the text, questions that biblical scholarship can help answer.

Baptist preaching will be biblical preaching; for we are a biblical people with a biblicist tradition, and we expound scripture with intellectual rigor and evangelical zeal.

(4) As evangelical preachers we preach for personal decision. The primacy of preaching's appeal is for personal relationship with Christ, to follow Christ and to receive him into our lives. We preach more than doctrine about Christ or about God; we preach the *person* of *Christ*, born into this world, teacher and healer, crucified and risen. Baptist preaching is also evangelical in its missionary reach to the world. Finally it is evangelical in the centrality of Christ and his gospel. We are gospel preachers with Christ's life, death, resurrection and present spirit at the heart of our preaching.

(5) Baptist preaching cares about the life of the community as well as the life of the individual. We not only help individuals open the Bible and interpret it for their life, we help the congregation as congregation open the Bible and let it guide its common life and faith. We train the people to interpret scripture *as* a congregation *for* the congregation, all the while honoring individual and dissenting interpretations.

(6) As part of a dissenting minority perspective, baptist preaching is a *counter-cultural act.* Our speech is a kind of poetic speech that offers new hope to a world trapped in the royal prose of the "powers that be." The prophetic/poetic speech, to use Brueggemann's words, "construes an alternative world," a world beyond the one we have taken for granted; and it offers "an evangelical world: an existence

shaped by the news of the gospel." It combats the official prose that has become an ideology of right or of left, "closed, managed, useful truth," useful to those in power but that, in fact, is a distortion of reality and denies the justice, grace and peace of the kingdom of God.[9]

(a) *Baptist preaching is bold to take on governmental or ecclesial authorities.* Thomas Helwys, early baptist preacher and founder of the first baptist congregation on English soil, went to see King James I to show him his treatise on religious liberty. As a member of the aristocracy Helwys thought he might have a chance to get an audience with the King, but James I was not about to entertain any form of dissent. Instead, Helwys wrote the following words to the King in the cover of his book, *The Mistery of Iniquity*, and sent it to him:

> The King is a mortall man and not God, therefore hath no power over ye immortall soules of his subjects to make laws and ordinances for them and to set spirituall Lords over them.
> If the King have authority to make spiritual Lords and lawes, then he is immortall God and not a mortall man. . . . God save ye King.[10]

The appeal was bold enough to have Helwys thrown into Newgate prison where he died.

Helwys has a noble line of baptist successors who have been unafraid to take on authorities and have suffered for their stand: John Bunyan, Roger Williams, Martin Luther King.

Baptist preaching is a counter-cultural act unafraid to take on the way truth, morality, and justice are handled by majority culture and the power structures of society. Baptist preaching builds up the church, which is itself a counter-cultural society, a community that lives as a parable of the kingdom.

(b) *Baptist preaching combines the personal gospel and the social gospel.* It is Billy Graham, Walter Rauschenbusch, George Truett, Lottie Moon, and Martin Luther King, Jr. Personal regeneration and social transformation are both goals of baptist preaching. We must not be made to choose.

E. Stanley Jones, a great Methodist, put it best in words akin to the following: The personal gospel without the social gospel is a soul without a body; the social gospel without the personal gospel is a body without a soul. One is a ghost, the other is a corpse.

Church growth experts say that one should never preach on social issues. That'll kill church growth, they say. That is also half a gospel, just as is preaching that tries to convert society while ignoring the conversion of the individual.

(c) *Baptist preaching reads scripture and life with a special eye for the weak and the powerless, the poor and marginalized.* We were born as a persecuted minority, and we watch out for other minorities.

We must not cozy up to the "powers that be" but find solidarity with those on the bottom rungs of society. Our hermeneutics of suspicion will be careful not to read scripture to support oppression but to read it in light of the God of Exodus and of the Christ who had no place to lay his head. We not only speak truth to power, we speak truth alongside the powerless.

# Conclusion

For the baptist Christian, scripture is the great ocean revealing the mystery of God. "Our only creed is the Bible," we say as we stand on its shore. We travel across its waters on a ship called the church, with every passenger's life and voice included. Christ is the captain of the ship leading us across its waters, and everything we learn of the righteousness and mercy of God becomes urgent good news for the world.

## Notes

[1]James William McClendon, Jr., *Systematic Theology: Ethics* (Nashville: Abingdon Press, 1986) 17-35.

[2]Gerard Manley Hopkins, "Pied Beauty," *The Poems of Gerard Manley Hopkins* (Oxford: Oxford Press, 1970) 70.

[3]I adapted the phrase of David Steinmetz as cited by William Willimon in Willimon's *Acts* (Atlanta: John Knox Press, 1988) 103.

[4]These phrases have been described especially well in E.Y. Mullins' *The Axioms of Religion* (Philadelphia: The Griffith & Rowland Press, 1908) and in H.W. Tribble's updating of Mullins' book, *The Baptist Faith* (Nashville: Convention Press, 1935).

[5]Cited in *The Baptist Way of Life*, Brooks Hays and John E. Steely (New Jersey: Prentice-Hall, Inc., 1963) 167.

[6]Ibid., 162.

[7]Thomas McKibbens, *The Forgotten Heritage: A Lineage of Great Baptist Preaching* (Macon: Mercer University Press).

[8]Ibid., 14.

[9]Walter Brueggemann, *Finally Comes a Poet: Daring Speech for Proclamation* (Minneapolis: Fortress Press, 1989) 2-4.

[10]Cited in McKibbens, 6.

# The Gospel Baptists Preach from the Bible

## George R. Beasley-Murray

Baptists are not distinguished from other Christians by a special view of the Bible that no one else holds. Nor are they marked off from other churches by preaching a gospel that no one else believes. On the contrary, they seek to be faithful to the apostolic gospel of Christ crucified and risen for the life of the world. Without in the least maligning others who hold to the evangelical faith, Baptists have been and are characterized by a living faith in Christ, confessed in baptism, and an eagerness to share that faith with all in the world.

One very important summary of that gospel preached by the apostles occurs in Hebrews 9:27-28:

> And just as it is appointed for mortals to die once, and after that the judgment, so Christ, having been offered once to bear the sins of many, will appear a second time, not to deal with sin, but to save those who are eagerly waiting for him.

As the title suggests, this sermon focuses on the gospel Baptists find in the Bible rather than a Baptist view of the Bible. As the text on which it is based, the sermon has two propositions: "The Christ of God is our Hope," and "Apart from Christ there is no hope."

The first proposition needs no demonstration for Christians. Christianity is Christ, and all who put their trust in him have a sure and certain hope, for hope is simply faith directed to the future. To trust in Jesus in this present life is to trust him for eternity, for he who died for our sins rose to be Lord of God's eternal kingdom of salvation, and moreover he pledged that he will in God's own time return to give us a share in that kingdom. Whether people accept or deny that hope is their problem. So far as we are concerned, that is where we stand, and we yield to no one on it.

The second statement—"There is no hope apart from Christ"—is not unnaturally disputed in the non-Christian world. That's not to be wondered at, for as Emil Brunner observed, "What oxygen is for the lungs, such is hope for the meaning of human life."[1] Without oxygen a human being cannot live, and without hope there is little reason to live. Consequently, all kinds of hopes are set before people as reasons for and means of attaining a worthwhile life. Paul in his day said that there were many gods and many lords of the souls of men, and there are many in our time, too. Most that held sway in Paul's age long ago crumbled in the dust. The same is always happening. People have been pinning their hopes on forceful leaders who advocate all kinds of creeds, philosophies, political systems, economic panaceas, dreams of utopias fashioned by human beings, and the like. One by one the idols totter as cataclysmic events shatter their clay feet. Some of the fallen idols admittedly get propped up, and painted up, and placed in fresh temples for the admiration of the multitudes. People grow disillusioned, however. These creatures hold no real hope. Consequently some persons come to believe that there is no hope anywhere.

In my younger years we had in England a gifted popularizer of atheistic science, H. G. Wells. He was not actually a scientist, but he had an ability to write. After a short period of flirting with the Christian faith he poured scorn on it. In his aging years he forsook his arrogance and became oppressed with black despair. He had come to believe that the death knell of humanity was sounding and, people being what they were, nothing could stop their destruction. He wrote:

> Our world of self-delusion will admit nothing of that. . . . It will perish amidst its evasions and fatuities. It is like a convoy lost in darkness on an unknown rocky coast, with quarrelling pirates in the chartrooms and savages clambering up the sides of the ships to plunder and do evil as the whim may take them. Mind near exhaustion still makes its final futile movement towards some way out or round or through the impasse. There is no way out or round or through.[2]

In face of the false hopes held out to humankind and the hopelessness of the pessimists, we proclaim the Christ of God as the one all-sufficient hope of humankind who is able to meet the needs of our age as of all ages. Indeed, that statement is not quite good enough, for the good news of God is not simply that Christ can meet our deepest need, but that he has met it. This he did when he redeemed us from our sin through his death and unleashed Life into the world through his resurrection. That process he will conclude by a last great act, when through the power of his Life he will destroy the death of the world.

Such is the theme of our text. It declares that a single and sufficient means of taking away the guilt of the world has been achieved by Christ. Deliverance from the crippling power of evil has been wrought, and by a culminating manifestation of his power in the future the age-long hope of humanity will find total realization in the completion of the kingdom that he brought by his life, death, and resurrection. Those assertions require to be spelled out, and that we shall proceed to do.

First, *Christ has decisively and effectively dealt with the sin of humanity by his death and resurrection.* This is a major concern of the author of the letter to the Hebrews, from which our text has been taken. To make it plain the writer contrasts the effectiveness of the sacrifice of Jesus with the ineffectiveness of the multitudinous sacrifices offered on Jewish and pagan altars.

Here, however, we must pause. This is a crucial issue for the biblical writers, yes. But has it any relation to the thought of people in our time? They are not particularly worried about their sins, and who among them ever gives a thought to sacrifices for sins?

That depends on the sins—and on the sacrifices they precipitate.

Unquestionably, sin has been banished from the vocabulary of modern folk. As a Canadian asserted to me in a conversation, "Sin is out! The sooner you preachers recognize it the better!" I told him that such was a curious statement for one to make who belonged to the generation that had witnessed unparalleled suffering inflicted on other human beings alike in peace and in war. Sin may have been banished from the modern consciousness, but conscience refuses to be silenced. Significantly, the most characteristic expression of the age that has lost sin is *Angst* (i.e. anxiety). That is attested by our mental hospitals and psychiatrists' consulting rooms. Thrown out of the front door, sin has slipped in by another, and in revenge has taken possession of the house. Karl Heim, a noted theologian, philosopher, and scientist, once cited the German poet Schiller as saying, "Of all evils, the greatest is the sense of sin." Heim agreed, and wrote a remarkable commentary on those words.

> Only guilt is the absolute evil, the absolutely fearful and unbearable thing, the plainly incurable injury. Everything else that is terrible in the world weighs light over against this. If one were to lay guilt in the balance and in the other all the other sufferings of the world—an unhappy love affair that makes life a hell, life-long forced labor in the mountain works of Siberia, years long and hopeless suffering from cancer with the only prospect of a tormented end, softening of the brain that leads to

madness, epilepsy with increasing imbecility—even so the balance on
which guilt lies would sink down to the depths, and the other balance
on which all the rest of suffering lies would quickly rise in the air. . . .
The future hell will be nothing other than a bad conscience.[3]

In reality sin is something that a human being cannot get rid of.
It's too big for us; it's too close to us; it's under our skin; it's deep in
our soul; it has eaten into our very being, like a cancer that we cannot
control.

Sin continues to demand its sacrifices. Pagan worshipers offered
beasts for their sins. What rivers of blood have flowed on a million
altars, but in vain! The Jew with a better revelation only had better
beasts to offer—"clean" beasts. This, too, as the writer to the Hebrews
said, was vain: "It is impossible for the blood of bulls and goats to
take away sins" (Heb 10:4). In modern times sinful humanity makes
a different kind of offering: We sacrifice our fellow human beings, and
that intensifies our plight.

Some years ago my wife, a friend, and I traveled by car from
Switzerland to Dunkirk, where they were to take a boat to England.
Having made good progress to our goal in Belgium we stopped in the
evening sun, in truly English fashion, for a rest and a cup of tea.
Waiting for a kettle to boil, I looked around and saw that we had
stopped outside a military cemetery. I wandered in and was confronted by a field of wooden crosses. Reading some of the names inscribed
on them, I saw that they were all Germans—thousands of them,
buried in the glory of their manhood in World War I. The opposite
side of the road had a similar appearance, and there I found another
cemetery, containing the remains of multitudes of British Tommies.
They had been men of my father's generation, and all had died, each
for his own land, and for peace and justice. My father was killed in
that war, a mere youngster in his twenties, hardly having lived, and
I never knew him. "A war to end war," they used to call it, but that
was a hope destined to be ground in dust.

We drove on after tea through the plain approaching Dunkirk. I
had not realized before how flat and how devoid of trees it was. Our
Swiss friend chatted on, failing to perceive that we two Britishers had
relapsed into silence, for we were vividly reminded of the terrible
retreat of the British army that had fled this way in World War II to
escape across the English Channel on a flotilla of boats that was
hastily assembled. But what was that army compared with the millions of men, women, and children who suffered and perished in

those war years? What has been the harvest of their unimaginable agonies? Worldwide peace? Reconciliation of the nations? The golden age of earlier hopes? To ask such questions is a mockery of the dead.

Against the background of the blood-stained alters of guilty humankind and the fields of those slain in battle there towers a solitary cross that spells out hope for the world: the Cross on which the Son of God gave himself as a ransom for all. Hard by it stands an empty tomb, open to the sky, for that self-same Son of God rose to transform by the power of his endless life those for whom he died. In life he had yielded a perfect obedience to God; by his death he perfectly affirmed that will, a will that willed not only holiness but also the annihilation of sin. In death Christ rendered to God the holiness demanded and bore the judgment of God on sin. So offered, the sacrifice was complete. Rejected by those he came to save, he was exalted by God—raised, not alone to life but to the throne of God, to the Lordship of the universe, to be the deliverer of all, a Savior for you, and Savior for me, a Savior for the world.

This man is my Savior! I saw in him my Deliverer. I sought and found his forgiveness. He broke the shackles that were my sins. He gave me his life. He holds me by his power. He will keep me to his heavenly kingdom. Is he your Deliverer too?

That leads me to consider *the power of the last act of Christ.* "He will appear a second time . . . to bring salvation to those who are waiting for him." He will "appear." That is a suggestive word to denote the Lord's coming. It pictures not so much the movement of the Lord from one point to another—from heaven to earth—as his stepping from behind a curtain. That is not wholly amiss. The closest parallel we possess to the second advent of Christ is his resurrection on Easter Sunday, when Jesus *appeared* from the realm of the dead as the conqueror of death. He did not need to travel far to appear to Mary, the apostles, Thomas, and the rest! But he "departed" at the ascension. In what sense can it be said that the risen Lord, who promised to be with us all the days, is absent from us? In two ways: though present with us, he is hidden from us; and though he occupies with the Father the throne of the universe, he restrains his hand. The last advent will witness the removal of those limitations. Our Lord will show himself, and he will show his hand. He will come in the glory of God, and he will work in the might of God.

The "work" of the returning Lord is the important thing about his second advent, for he is to bring to realization what humankind has yearned for but has never been able to achieve, despite claims from time to time to have accomplished it.

When I first visited Rome, one of my colleagues urged me to be sure to see the Ara Pacis, the Altar of Peace. After much searching, I finally found it by the tomb of the emperor of Augustus. From the point of view of history and of art, it is a highly significant work, but my interest in it lay in other directions. That altar embodied the rival hope that was to struggle with the Christian hope for two and a half centuries, until at last the "rival" died, a lie slain by the truth. Augustus was the first Roman emperor to adopt and adapt the ancient Egyptian belief in the king as a god to be venerated by his people. By his time it had become a firmly messianic idea—the emperor was the bringer of the golden age of ancient dreams, the Savior of the world. Augustus actually believed that he had brought that golden age of peace to the world, and he celebrated its establishment by erecting the Altar of Peace. His successors increasingly pressed similar claims. Nero boasted that, in fulfillment of the hope that the creatures would submit themselves to a human, even the birds of the palace gardens chanted "Hail Caesar." It was perfectly true, for they were imperial parrots, trained to do precisely that. By every means the endeavor was made to perpetuate the lie, which everybody repeated but few believed, till at length it was killed by the emperors themselves as they bowed the knee to Jesus, the true and only Savior, and confessed him to be the Lord of the world, the King of the kings of the earth.

The Christian hope must never be confused with the empty claims made by rulers and demagogues through the centuries, for the Christ of Golgotha is the Lord of Easter. To him all work of judgment and salvation has been committed by the Father. He is to raise the dead, judge the world and bestow one everlasting kingdom—works that God alone can do and that God in Christ has sworn that he shall do. We believe that what he has promised he is able also to perform.

In light of the certainty both of the judgment and the kingdom of Christ, the author of Hebrews appeals: "Do not throw away your confidence, but hold on to the end!" (10:35-36). That is, "Keep your joy and fearlessness of faith! Resist every temptation to let it go!" And he adds, "For we are not people who shrink back and lose all, but we are of those who keep their souls."

By the grace of God we would make that confession of faith ours. We will not number ourselves with those who "lose heart and lose God." We belong rather to the company of those who maintain faith in God against all odds. Hebrews 11 recites the famous roll call of heroes of faith as examples of how to do precisely that. We therefore belong to the company of Noah, Abraham and the patriarchs, Moses, David, the prophets, the apostles; the martyrs and confessors of the church of our Lord Jesus Christ; those who kept the flame of truth alive like Athanasius, Augustine and St. Francis; Luther, Calvin, and their fellow Reformers;  Smyth, Helwys, and the early Baptist pioneers; Wesley, Carey, Spurgeon, and a host of other preachers of the gospel. We belong, indeed, to the saints of God in all the earth today, including and especially the saints of God in our Baptist communities scattered throughout the globe. We belong to *them!*

I am told that after the attempt on Adolf Hitler's life in 1944 the famous German Christian Leader, Bishop Lilje, was put in prison in Berlin. The Allied air raids were mounting in that time. When the sirens used to sound and the guards went below to the shelters, the bishop in his cell on the upper floor of the building would go to the window and knock down the blackout curtaining in order to look up at the stars. With despots below and hell about to break loose about him, he looked up and received afresh grace to endure.

"Therefore, since we are surrounded by so great a cloud of witnesses, let us also lay aside every weight and the sin that clings so closely, and let us run with perseverance the race that is set before us, *fixing our eyes on Jesus*" (Heb 12:1-2 personal).

## Notes

[1]Emil Brunner, *Eternal Hope* (London: Lutterworth Press, 1954) 7.

[2]H. G. Wells, *Mind At The End of Its Tether* (London: Wm. Heinemann, 1945) 15.

[3]Karl Heim, *Jesus, The World's Perfector* (Edinburgh: Oliver and Boyd, 1959) 6-7.

# Baptists, the Bible,
# and Authority

## *Hugh Wamble*

There is a lively interest among Southern Baptists at present in the crucial subject of Scripture and authority. Many voices have been raised—from the shrill falsetto of passionate emotion to the dull drone of dispassionate reason. Being a Baptist, I have a native interest in the subject. Being a student of Baptist history, I am justified in speaking on the subject, "Baptists, the Bible and Authority." However, my studies have revealed such variety as to make me question numerous pontifications about uniformity on the subject. There is a cause to fear the consequences of the dangerous, non-Baptist notion that there has been and must now be uniformity. In the alchemy of history, this notion distills into dogma, and ecclesiasticism becomes its guardian.

I offer evidence, drawn from official records (mostly confessions of faith) which stretch across three and a half centuries, regarding "our historic position" relative to the Scripture. It is my hope to make the evidence relevant to Baptist life today. Perhaps you would prefer to do your own study on the subject. This I commend. Anyone may go to the records for himself. Only two prior conditions are necessary: (1) a genuine interest in our historic position, and (2) a willingness to come under the inhibiting influence of information.[1]

## I. Identification

Several terms have been used in Baptist confessions to identify Scripture.

(1) *Bible:* Though common today, "Bible" was comparatively late in finding recognition in Baptist confessions, the first being the New Connexion General Baptist articles of 1770. Derived from the Latin term, *biblia,* meaning "the books," it goes back to the Middle Ages and has been common among Roman Catholics. The Latin Vulgate,

officially approved as the authentic Catholic version by the Council of Trent in 1546, has appeared in various editions under the title *Biblia Sacra.* The term "Bible" was used by Protestant reformers, but not extensively, except for the title of published editions of the Scripture.[2] Following the publication of the Authorized Version, it was normally used in the seventeenth century to refer to a particular edition.[3] Early in the eighteenth century, Pietism popularized the term among Lutherans. The Wesleyan revival, out of which the New Connexion General Baptists evolved, aided its popularity in England. By 1800 it was widely used. It appears in the revised edition of *The Baptist Catechism* of 1794.[4] It is now the best known term around the world especially among non-Christians, due in part to the work of numerous Bible societies.

The competition of names may be seen in the New Hampshire confession of 1830–1833. True to older Protestant idiom, it entitles its article "Of the Scriptures." Then, true to newer idiom, it discusses "the Holy Bible." It does not use the term "Scripture."[5]

Fundamentalist confessions of the twentieth century show a decided preference for the term "Bible." One fundamentalist group has named itself the Baptist Bible Union. Such adjectives as Bible-loving, Bible-believing, Bible-preaching are common.

(2) *Scripture:* The preferred name in Baptist confessions is "Scripture," with its variations. It occurs in all major confessions of the formative seventeenth century and in most subsequent confessions. However, some modern statements, coming from certain Fundamentalist circles, seem to prefer such terms as "Bible" and "Word."

The preference for "Scripture" is rooted in the Reformation. Luther wanted to be known as "Doctor of Holy Scripture." Other Protestants preferred it, and it was the most common term among English reformers, as is abundantly evident in their confessions and writings.

The Baptist preference for it may be seen in their two longest confessions of the seventeenth century: the Particular Baptist confession of 1677 and the General Baptists' *An Orthodox Creed* of 1678/9. Both are heavily indebted to the Westminster confession of Presbyterians (1646-1648), with the 1677 confession showing most Presbyterian influence. The first chapter of the 1677 confession is entitled "Of the Holy Scriptures";[6] the 37th article of *An Orthodox Creed* (1678/9) is entitled "Of the sacred Scripture."[7] It should be noted that no Baptist confession has an article entitled "On the Word of God" or "On the Bible." In the Reformed tradition, or Continental Presbyterianism, however, the first article of the influential Second Helvetic Confession (1566) is entitled "Of the Holy Scripture Being the True Word of God." The 1677 confession uses "Scripture" and related terms twenty-nine times, compared to thirteen uses of "Word" to mean Scripture. *An Orthodox Creed* uses "Scripture" sixteen times and "Word" thirteen times, but its article on the Scripture uses "scripture" six times, compared to only one occurrence of "Word."

The preference of Particular Baptists, the ancestors of American Baptists, can best be seen in the preface. Written as an explanatory introduction, not as a doctrinal statement, it reflects the common usage of the period. Only "Scripture" is used—six times. Particular Baptists affirmed their consent with Presbyterians, Congregationalists and other orthodox Protestants "in all the fundamental articles of the Christian religion." They explained that they readily acquiesced "in that form of sound words which hath been, in consent with the holy scriptures, used by others before us," in order to declare "our hearty agreement with them, in that wholesome protestant doctrine, which, with so clear evidence of scriptures, they have asserted." They also appropriated the language of Presbyterians, as they explain in a picturesque phrase, in order "to convince all that we have no itch to clog religion with new words." They took care, they explained, "to affix texts of scripture in the margin, for the confirmation of each article in our Confession," and commended the "example of the noble Bereans, who searched the scriptures daily that they might find out whether the things preached to them were so or not."[8]

(3) *Word:* The term "Word" or "Word of God" appears frequently in Baptist confessions—but not always as Scripture. There are several different meanings, often appearing in the same confession.

(a) One meaning is *Son of God*, the second person of the Trinity: the "Son is the everlasting Word of the Father, and his wisdom";[9] "there are THREE which beare record in heaven, the FATHER, the WORD, and the Spirit";[10] "as one congregacion hath CHRIST, so hath all. . . . And the Word off GOD cometh not out from anie one, neither to anie one congregacion in particuler";[11] "He took to Him the shape of a servant, the Word became flesh";[12] "this infinite Being is set forth to be the Father, the Word, and the Holy Spirit; and these three agree in one";[13] "this God. . . did. . .create all things, by, and for Jesus Christ; . . . who is the word of God. . .and upholds all things by the word of his power";[14] "In this divine and infinite Being there are three subsistences, the Father the Word (or Son) and Holy Spirit";[15] "the Son of God, or the eternal word, is very and true God."[16]

The preferred proof-texts for this usage are John 1 and John 5. No confession cites Revelation 19:13ff. on this point. In fact, Revelation is not cited very much in Baptist confessions. For example, only eleven of the 754 New Testament references in the 1677 confession came from Revelation.

(b) In a few instances "Word" means *Gospel* or preaching: "to preach the word, or gospel, to the world of unbelievers";[17] "faith is ordinarily begot by the preaching of the Gospel, or word of Christ";[18] "repentance and faith are wrought in the hearts of men, by the preaching of the word, outwardly in the Scriptures."[19] Phrases like "preaching the Word" and "ministry of the Word" are common. One confession uses the phrase "the word preached," and also calls sacraments or ordinances a "visible word."[20]

(c) The most frequent meaning of "Word of God" in Baptist confessions is *Scripture*. Only three seventeenth-century English Baptist confessions—the English *Declaration* of 1611, *Propositions and Conclusions* of 1612 and *The True Gospel-Faith* of 1654, all of which are General Baptist statements—fail to use it in this sense. In some confessions "Word" is repeatedly used to mean Scripture: four times in the 1644 confession, thirteen times in the 1677 confession and thirteen times in *An Orthodox Creed*.

This usage has a long history in evangelical circles. In his running battle with Romanism, John Wyclif, the harbinger of the Reformation, used "Word of God" to mean Scripture, but he preferred the term "Scripture," as evidenced by the title of a major book, *De Veritate Scripturae*. According to Protestant reformers, true churches (evangelical) are to be distinguished from false churches (Catholic) by two marks: faithful preaching of the Word and proper administration of the sacraments.

Zwingli was the first of the reformers to make much of "Word of God," but the term became common in the Protestant idiom. In *Of the Clarity and Certainty or Power of the Word of God* (1522), Zwingli manifests typical Protestant ambiguity about the use of "Word" in relation to Scripture: sometimes as written Word, sometimes as spoken word based on Scripture and sometimes as the effect of evangelical preaching. Through the effective working of the Holy Spirit, the written Word becomes the living Word of God, with power to give inward enlightenment and assurance.[21]

This ambiguity appears throughout Protestantism. Two Particular Baptist confessions—of 1644 and of 1677—tacitly acknowledge it by calling Scripture the "written" Word: "Under the Name of Holy

Scripture, or the Word of God written: are now contained all the Books of the Old and New Testament."[22]

In briefer confessions of the nineteenth and twentieth centuries, whose sloganic, shibbolethic character represents a departure from earlier confessions, there is a noticeable tendency to identify Scripture as "Word of God."[23] Fundamentalist confessions of the twentieth century tend to reserve "Word of God" to mean Scripture only, never using it in confessions to mean the Son of God.[24]

The changed meaning of the term appears in stark relief in the following contrast. In 1611 Baptist refugees in Holland stated that "the scriptures off the Old and New Testament" ought to be searched "for they testifie off CHRIST" and ought therefore "to be vsed withall reverence, as conteyning the Holie Word off God."[25] In 1923 the Fundamentalist Baptist Bible Union emphatically asserted that "THE HOLY BIBLE . . . as originally written, does not contain and convey the word of God, but IS the very Word of God."[26]

The Southern Baptist Convention has recently passed a motion identifying "the *entire* Bible as the authoritative, authentic, infallible Word of God"—with emphasis on "entire." As originally presented, the motion implies that the identification, as stated, is "our historic position."[27] This is not the case, however. Only one confession—Sandy Creek (1816)—uses either of these adjectives ("infallible") in connection with "Word of God."

The historic position of Baptists is to use "Word of God" to mean any number of things: Scripture, Son of God, Gospel, evangelical preaching and "the Word in our Hearts."[28] Because of its exclusive use of the term to mean Scripture, the 1962 motion is, therefore, less faithful to "our historic position" than the opening sentence of the presidential address to the Convention in 1951, delivered by one who would not admit to being a liberal on this or any other point: ". . . to manifest the Incarnate Word from the written Word by the spoken word."[29]

## II. Inspiration

Baptist confessions are indefinite about the inspiration of Scripture. The *fact* of inspiration is assumed and affirmed, but the *manner* of inspiration receives little attention—until recent generations.

The fact of inspiration is affirmed in such expressions as "given by inspiration of the holy Ghost,"[30] "given by inspiration of God,"[31] record of Jesus Christ "given of him by god in scripture,"[32] "God (who is truth it self) the Author thereof,"[33] "delivered by the Spirit"[34] and "of Divine inspiration."[35]

On the subject of the manner of inspiration, confessions are usually silent. There is considerable variety among the few confessions which deal in any way with the method of inspiration. An enigmatic explanation appears in the Smyth group's confession, patterned after a Waterlander Mennonite statement: ". . . described by the Holy Ghost, of Paul."[36] Though trying to show the fullest possible agreement with Waterlanders, the Smyth group deliberately altered a Waterlander statement suggesting the dictation theory of inspiration: "as in the words of Paul (Rom 13:1-3), the Holy Spirit dictating."[37] This suggests, of course, that the English Baptist group did not hold the dictation theory.

The Somerset confession of 1656 uniquely relates the Scripture's origin to the Son's prophetic office: "As he is our prophet, so he hath given us the scriptures, the Old and New Testament." The Holy Spirit's work is to teach, open and reveal "the mysteries of the kingdom, and will of God unto us."[38]

The first Baptist confession to offer an explanation of the manner of inspiration is the New Hampshire confession (1830–1833) which says that "the Holy Bible was written by men divinely inspired."[39] This implies the dynamic theory of inspiration: God inspires and reveals his will to individuals who then express his revelation in keeping with their own backgrounds and personalities.

In the last quarter of the nineteenth century, however, the mechanical theory became popular among some ultra-conservatives and was affirmed by certain Fundamentalist and Landmark groups. For example, the American Baptist Association expresses belief in "the infallible verbal inspiration of the whole Bible."[40] The North American Baptist Association affirms belief in "the infallibility and plenary verbal inspiration of the Scriptures."[41] In keeping with the Fundamentalist notion that God must operate above and contrary to the natural order, not in and through it, the Baptist Bible Union (1923) changed the New Hampshire phrase "written by men divinely inspired" to "written by men supernaturally inspired." To prevent any misunderstanding it also added an explanatory note:

> 2. By "INSPIRATION" we mean that the books of the Bible were written by holy men of old, as they were moved by the Holy Spirit, in such a definite way that their writings were supernaturally inspired and

free from error, as no other writings have ever been or ever will be inspired.[42]

Some contend that the plenary verbal theory is the historic position of Baptists regarding inspiration, and they sometimes appeal to two confessional statements to prove it. The most common, but latest as to time of appearance, is the New Hampshire phrase "truth, without any mixture of error, for its matter." Some understand "matter" to mean words and facts. However, it refers to the character of Scriptures as "a perfect treasure of heavenly instruction," a revelation of "the principles by which God will judge us" and "the supreme standard" in religion.[43] In the philosophy of Peter Ramus, on which Puritan theology and this phrase were based, there is a sharp distinction between "form" (including words) and "matter" (content).

The second, but earliest as to time, comes from the 1677 or Philadelphia confession, taken over directly from the Westminster confession of Presbyterians:

> The Old Testament in *Hebrew*, (which was the Native language of the people of God of old) and the New Testament in *Greek*, (which at the time of writing of it was most generally known to the Nations being immediately inspired by God, and by his singular care and Providence kept pure in all Ages, are therefore authentical; . . .[44]

The article in which this statement appears is concerned with the need to translate Scripture "into the vulgar language of every nation." It therefore places emphasis on the texts which are to be used in the work of translation. The Roman Catholic Council of Trent in 1546 authorized the Latin Vulgate as the authentic text. Protestants, on the other hand, insisted on going back to the original languages (not "original manuscripts" or "autographs," which modern Fundamentalists talk about) for judging "all controversies of Religion" as well as for translation. It may also be noted that, whereas modern Fundamentalism appeals back to non-extant autographs and only emphasizes inspiration, the Particular Baptists of the seventeenth century united preservation ("kept pure in all Ages") with inspiration ("being immediately inspired by God"), and contended that Hebrew and Greek texts as received are the authentic norm.

Some improperly seek a clue to the meaning of the 1677 statement in the views of certain mid-seventeenth century Calvinists of Switzerland and Holland, such as the following. Cocceius (d. 1669) said that "men of God . . . were God's assistants and amanuenses who wrote exactly as they spoke, not by their own will but driven by the H. Spirit."[45] Voetius (d. 1676) said that New Testament writers thought and wrote in Greek "by the inspiration and dictation of the H. Spirit" and contended that Greek accents "unmistakably belong not only to the elegance of the language and script but also to its integrity at that time."[46] A Swiss Reformed council of 1675 adopted *Formula consensus ecclesiarum Helveticarum*, which asserts the theory that Hebrew vowel points, as well as things and words, were "God-inspired."

English Protestants were acquainted with the Continental controversy provoked by such verbalists. However, few Englishmen favored the plenary verbal theory. In 1722 some English officials urged the abolition of *Formula consensus ecclesiarum Helveticarum* as a prerequisite to peace and unity among Protestants.

*An Orthodox Creed* (1678/9) of General Baptists, who were more biblicistic than Particular Baptists, completely omits any reference to pure texts. This is significant, in view of the fact that it shows obvious kinship with the Westminster article on Scripture in several other matters. Why this omission? The answer is suggested in Thomas Grantham's introduction to *Christianismus Primitivus* in 1678, the year of *An Orthodox Creed*. There has arisen "a generation of Men," Grantham said, "to quarrel the Oracles, on which the Christian Faith hath so far a dependance, as if they prove False, Christianity cannot be true." "These kind of Men talk much of the *Originals*, as if nothing else would down with them but the *Original Text*." Though the controversy was largely among non-Baptists, Grantham noted that "the Baptized Churches" are not "without Learned Men" who "have concern'd themselves in this Controversie." Apparently, however, Baptists did not favor the novel theory of absolute inspiration and pure transmission of original texts.

No original text is extant, Grantham said. He expressed the judgment that

> it was better for the Churches, that these first Sheets should not endure long, the same Matter* being now committed to Writing by many Hands throughout the whole world; for had any now these first Draughts to shew, they might abuse the World, and all the Churches in the World, more than any Man can do by the Copies; as by adding or taking away at pleasure.

Grantham was concerned for doctrinal content, not textual form:

. . . [W]hy might not these Copyists possibly vary in some word or tittle, and yet these Sacred Writings never the worse, while the Holy Doctrine therein was not violated? Can we think that when the Apostles preached, they still had the self-same Phrases? This were idle to imagin, and yet they had the self-same Gospel to preach in every place. I speak not this as that I approve of altering the Holy Writings, no not in the least *iota;* yet if casually in Transcribing or Printing there should be some failure, I do not think by and by that Copy is to be rejected altogether, or the Authority of the Scripture therefore made null or void. . . .

The "matter" or "Holy Doctrine" is not affected by textual variations, according to Grantham:

. . . [T]his I declare to all the World, that I conceive it abundantly satisfactory, that the Copies of the Sacred Oracles, commonly called the Originals, have no corrupt Doctrine in them. . . . And besides, it is certainly impossible (in these days) for any Man whatsoever to corrupt the Greek Copies, there are so many Copies extant to discover the Cheat. . . .We therefore conclude that such hath been the Providence of God, that Men could not corrupt these Holy Writings

by erasing or inserting "so much as one Sentence" without being detected. On this basis, Grantham claimed "ground to believe, that no material change hath befallen the Scripture since the Writing thereof to this day."[47]

A perfect text is not necessary. Biblical writers "did not write the Gospel with the same stile and exactness"; nor should "Interpreters" be expected to show "exactness in Translating the Gospel." "I am persuaded," Grantham declared, "I can find as seeming Contradictions, among the Evangelists, in penning the Divine Story, as any Man can find in the Translations which are extant." If "there were as great an harmony in Doctrine and Practice, among all that own the Christian Name, as there is among the several Translations," he predicted, "we should soon be one Church, for they are all one Scripture." Even "the meanest of our Translations" have "so much . . . Perfection" of doctrine, he claimed, "that I fear no Mans growth in Christian Vertue and Knowledg, comes up to the pitch of it."[48]

Throughout their history, Baptists have affirmed the fact of inspiration, but they have not erected a dogma about the manner of its inspiration. The Sunday School Board of the Southern Baptist Convention has recently signallized "the historic Baptist principle of the freedom of the individual to interpret the Bible for himself, to hold a particular theory of inspiration of the Bible which seems most reasonable to him, and to develop his beliefs in accordance with his theory." With this "historic Baptist principle" as a norm, it would seem that plenary verbalists who would impose their own theory on all are actually the ones who show infidelity to our heritage and threaten our historic position.

# III. Revelation

The uniqueness of the Scripture's inspiration is directly related to God's saving revelation, of which Scripture is the record.[49] As the 1677 confession says, neither "the light of Nature" nor "the works of Creation and Providence" can provide

> that knowledge of God and His will, which is necessary unto Salvation. Therefore it pleased the Lord at sundry times, and in divers manners, to reveal himself, and to declare that His will unto his Church; and after for the better preserving, and propagating of the Truth, and for the more sure Establishment and Comfort of the Church . . . to commit the same wholly unto writing; which maketh the Holy Scriptures to be most necessary, those former ways of Gods revealing his will unto his people being now ceased.[50]

*An Orthodox Creed* of General Baptists (1678/9) expresses a similar view, but with less emphasis on the Scripture as record:

> Nor yet do we believe, that the works of creation, nor the law written in the heart, viz. natural religion, as some call it, or the light within man, as such, is sufficient to inform man of Christ the mediator, or of the way to salvation, or eternal life by him; but the holy scriptures are necessary to instruct all men into the way of salvation, and eternal life.[51]

In 1946 the Southern Baptist Convention officially approved a statement which states that "the New Testament [is] the divinely inspired record and interpretation of the supreme revelation of God through Jesus Christ as Redeemer, Savior and Lord."[52] The Sunday School Board's recent *Curriculum Guide* is therefore in the best Baptist tradition in holding that "the Bible is the inspired record of God's revelation of himself and of his way and will for mankind."[53]

# IV. Relation between Faith and Scripture

There are two explanations in Baptist confessions regarding the relationship between faith and Scripture.

First, among those who tend to define faith as intellectual assent to propositional and factual truth, Scripture is the starting-point for faith. This is most evident among Waterlander Mennonites, who defined faith as "a most certain cognition or knowledge acquired through the grace of God from the sacred scriptures"[54] and contended that scriptural pronouncements on various doctrines (incarnation, generation, revelation, passion, death, cross, ascension, glorification and exaltation of Christ) "must be embraced with a faithful heart."[55] It is less evident among General Baptists. They omitted the latter article but showed some kinship with Waterlanders in their emphasis on faith as mental assent to Biblical doctrine: "true, living, working faith . . . is an assured understanding and knowledge of the heart, obtained out of the Word of God."[56] Later General Baptists also held this view: "a knowledge in the mind of the doctrine of the law and gospel contained in the prophetical, and apostolical scriptures of the Old and New Testament";[57] "assent to the truth of the Gospel."[58] However, General Baptists stopped short of the Mennonites' extreme emphasis on faith as mental assent. Justifying faith, they held, is of the heart[59] or in the soul.[60] They made a sharp distinction between "faith" and "justifying faith":

> Faith is an act of the understanding, giving a firm assent to the things contained in the holy scriptures. But justifying faith is a grace, or habit, wrought in the soul, by the holy ghost, through preaching the word of God, whereby we are enabled to believe, not only that the Messias is offered to us, but also to take and receive him, as a Lord and Savior, and wholly and only to rest upon Christ, for grace and eternal salvation.

Second, among those who tend to define faith as experience, Scripture confirms faith:

> Faith is the gift of God wrought in the hearts of the elect by the Spirit of God, whereby they come to see, know, and beleeve the truth of the Scriptures, & not onely so, but the excellencie of them above all other writings and things in the world, as they hold forth the glory of God in

his attributes, the excellency of Christ in his nature and offices, and the power of the fulnesse of the Spirit in its workings and operations; and thereupon are inabled to cast the weight of their soules upon this truth thus beleeved.[61]

By faith, which is the work of the Spirit, "a Christian believeth to be true, whatsoever is revealed in the Word" concerning the Trinity. Though an effect of one's faith is "to cast his Soul upon the truth thus believed," it is not the chief effect; "the principal acts of Saving Faith, have immediate relation to *Christ*, accepting, receiving, and resting upon him alone, for Justification, Sanctification, and Eternal Life, by virtue of the Covenant of Grace."[62]

The New Hampshire article on faith, added by J. Newton Brown in 1853 and adopted by the Southern Baptist Convention in 1925, defines faith without any tinge of intellectualism:

Repentance and Faith are sacred duties, and also inseparable graces, wrought in our souls by the regenerating Spirit of God; whereby being deeply convinced of our guilt, danger, and helplessness, and of the way of salvation by Christ, we turn to God with unfeigned contrition, confession, and supplication for mercy; at the same time heartily receiving the Lord Jesus Christ as our Prophet, Priest, and King, and relying on him alone as the only and all-sufficient Savior.[63]

Nevertheless, among Southern Baptists, these two views—faith as mental assent and faith as experience—are sometimes melded. For example, Southern Seminary's "Abstract of Principles" (1859) thus defines "Saving faith":

the belief, on God's authority, of whatsoever is revealed in His Word concerning Christ; accepting and resting upon Him alone for justification and eternal life. It is wrought in the heart by the Holy Spirit, and is accompanied by all other saving graces, and leads to a life of holiness.[64]

Contending that the Bible is historically accurate at all points, Fundamentalists and Landmarkers have demanded assent to Biblical evidence on various subjects, such as "the Genesis Account of Creation"[65] or "the Biblical account of creation." One group (Baptist Bible Union) claims the acceptance of "the sacred Scriptures upon these subjects at their face value:" the Bodily Resurrection, the Ascension, the High Priesthood, the Second Coming, the Resurrection of the Righteous Dead, the Change of the Living in Christ, On the Throne of David and His Reign on Earth.[66]

Despite current contentions, the Fundamentalist view of faith, which requires assent to and acceptance of Biblical evidence at every point, is not our historic Baptist position. What is our historic position? Actually, there are two aspects to it. First, in the "mental assent" tradition, faith does not pertain to all the details of Scripture, but only to Biblical doctrine, on such matters as "God, Christ, and other heavenly things," "law and gospel," "truth of the Gospel" and Jesus Christ "as a Lord and Savior."[67] Second, in the "experience" tradition, faith is concerned with the Scripture's evidence about the Father's attributes, the person and work of Jesus Christ, and the work of the Holy Spirit.[68]

## V. Method of Interpretation

Baptist confessions have very little to say about the method of interpretation—until recent generations. In recent months some Southern Baptists have suggested, but contrary to fact, that our historic position calls for the "literal" interpretation. Baptist confessions do not prescribe the "literal" approach.

Since Scriptures deal with "the whole Councel of God concerning all things necessary for his [God's] own Glory, Mans Salvation, Faith and life,"[69] interpretation is concerned with these matters, not with all literal details.

The primary and "infallible rule of interpretation of Scripture is the Scripture itself."[70] It "is the best interpreter of itself."[71] When there is "a question about the true and full sense of any Scripture," which suggests that some passages are not self-interpreting, "it must be searched by other places that speak more clearly."[72]

Whereas some things concerning God's glory and man's salvation are "expressely set down . . . in the *Holy Scripture*," others are only "necessarily contained" in it,[73] and ought therefore to be interpreted logically or "according to the analogy of faith"[74] or one's doctrinal system. These terms "necessarily contained" and "analogy of faith" are related to logical interpretation, not literal. A statement in a sermon of 1641, delivered either by William Kiffin or by Hanserd Knollys, illustrates this point:

> All Texts are to be understood literally, except they make against some other Scriptures, or except the very Coherence and Dependance of the Scripture shews it otherwise, or it makes against the Analogy of Faith.[75]

In the final analysis, a "saving understanding of such things as are revealed in the Word" is dependent on "the inward illumination of the spirit of God."[76] Since its end is salvation,[77] Scripture is not truly interpreted without the witness of the Spirit.

As for "those things which are necessary to be known, believed, and observed for Salvation," it takes no special training to interpret them; "not only the learned, but the unlearned, in a due use of ordinary means [common sense], may attain to a sufficient [saving] understanding of them," for they are "clearly propounded, and opened in some place of Scripture or other."[78]

A definite change from the foregoing appears in Fundamentalist confessions. Fundamentalists claim that the Bible must be interpreted literally. For example, "the Genesis account of creation," the Baptist Bible Union asserted, must "be accepted literally, and not allegorically or figuratively,"[79] and Biblical evidence on various subjects must be believed in and accepted "at their face and full value."[80]

Among Southern Baptists at present, there is a circular saw to the effect that "the Bible means what it says and says what it means." It is associated with the "literal" method. Despite its appeal to the ear, this slogan conveys some unfortunate implications: that the Bible is the easiest book of all to understand; that it is simple; that to read it is to understand it; that it does not have to be studied. The slogan is not a faithful representation of our historic position. The 1677 or Philadelphia confession, for example, shows much greater appreciation for the depth and mystery of the Scripture's message than the slogan. It says: "All things in Scripture are not alike plain in themselves, nor alike clear unto all."[81] Its supporting text is 2 Pet. 2:16.

> As also in all his [Paul's] epistles, speaking in them of these things: in which are some things hard to be understood, which they that are unlearned and unstable wrest, as they do also the other scriptures, unto their own destruction (ASV).

Thus, the slogan is faithful neither to Scripture nor to our historic position.

# VI. Authority of Scripture

The crucial issue concerns the nature of the Scripture's authority. With few exceptions, all of them coming from modern confessions issued by Fundamentalists and Landmarkers, Baptist confessions specify that religion is the area of the Scripture's authority. They do not claim for it authority and infallibility in other areas, nor do they claim that man is able to understand Scripture fully.

The Scripture's authority is authenticated by "the inward work of the Holy Spirit, bearing witness by and with the Word in our Hearts." Its authority depends "not upon the testimony of any man, or Church; but wholly upon God"; nor is its authority proven by numerous arguments regarding its internal excellencies.[82] As *The Baptist Catechism* expresses it,

> The Bible evidences itself to be God's Word by the heavenliness of its doctrine, the unity of its parts, its power to convert sinners and to edify saints; but the Spirit of God only, bearing witness by and with the Scriptures in our hearts, is able fully to persuade us that the Bible is the Word of God.[83]

The Scripture's authority is related to salvation as the following phrases indicate: all things "necessary for us to know, and to believe to salvation";[84] whatsoever is "needfull for us to know, beleeve, and acknowledge" concerning Christ;[85] "necessary to be known, believed, and observed for Salvation";[86] "all things necessary to be known for the salvation of men and women";[87] "all things necessary for salvation";[88] "all things necessary for his [God's] own Glory, Man's salvation";[89] "to make men wise unto salvation";[90] "a sufficient and infallible rule and guide to Salvation";[91] "salvation for its end."[92] The Scripture's infallibility relates, therefore, to salvation.

Specifically, the Scripture's authority in salvation deals with "God, Christ, and other heavenly things,"[93] "heavenly instruction,"[94] "the Nature and Office of Christ,"[95] "the glory of God in his attributes, the excellency of Christ in his nature and offices, and the power and fulnesse of the Spirit in its workings and operations."[96] One confession (1610) says, however, that neither works of creation nor "Holy Scriptures . . . intend to teach us what God is in substance or essence, but what He is in effect and property" or "only the hinder parts of God"; it also affirms that man's conformity to God's "effects and properties" or "His divine and heavenly attributes," not a mental or intellectual understanding of God, "is the true saving knowledge of God."[97] Several confessions say that God "as he is in himselfe" is incomprehensible to finite man, but they contend that enough can be known about him for salvation.[98]

In addition to its authoritativeness as to salvation, the Scripture's authority extends to matters of faith and practice: "its [it is] the Scriptures of the Prophets and Apostles that we square our faith and practice by . . . the rule of . . . faith and practice";[99] "a rule and direction unto us both for faith and practice";[100] "the rule whereby Saints both in matters of Faith and conversation [conduct] are to be regulated";[101] "the only rule, and square of our sanctification and obedience in all good works, and piety";[102] "serving to furnish the man of God for every good work";[103] "the rule of Faith and Life";[104] "the . . . only rule of faith and practice";[105] "the supreme and sufficient rule of our faith and practice";[106] "the infallible rule of faith and practice";[107] "the sole authority for faith and practice."[108]

Matters of practice include such things as moral conduct, "the worship and service of God, and all other Christian duties," [109] and walking "together in particular societies, or Churches."[110] It "reveals the principles by which God will judge us."[111] Though Scripture is normative for church life, there are yet

> some circumstances concerning the worship of God, the government of the Church common to humane actions and societies; which are to be ordered by the light of nature, and Christian prudence according to the general rules of the Word, which are always to be observed.[112]

In some unspecified matters, therefore, Scripture provides general principles, not specific commands and examples.

As authoritative in the area of religion, Scripture stands over and judges all other religious authorities, however named: "Decrees of Councels" and popes, "opinions of antient Writers" or any religious writer whatsoever, "Doctrines of men," "private Spirits" such as "pretended immediate inspirations, dreams, or prophetical predictions," "the law written in the heart," "the light within man" and "the works of creation."[113] It is "the supreme standard by which all human conduct, creeds, and [religious] opinions should be tried."[114] The authority of Scripture means, therefore, that all religious beliefs and practices, whatever they may be and wherever they may be found, must stand under judgment of Scripture.

Primary authority rests with the New Testament. The earliest Baptist confession (1610) says that the proper Christian doctrine for the government of Christ's spiritual kingdom, "so much as is needful for us to salvation," is written "in the Scripture of the New Testament, whereto we apply whatsoever we find in the canonical book of the

Old Testament, which hath affinity and verity."[115] Evidence for Baptists' acceptance of the superior authority of the New Testament may be found in Scripture references, inserted in text and margin, with which confessions are supported. For example, according to my own hurried tabulation, there are 945 Scripture references in the 1677 confession, the longest in Baptist history. The New Testament provides 754 and the Old Testament, 191. Over a fourth of the Old Testament references (54) comes from Psalms. The Pauline corpus provides about 46 per cent (346) of all New Testament references. The preferred book is Romans, with 108 citations; followed by the two Corinthian letters with 74, John with 64, Matthew and Acts with 53 each, and Ephesians with 50. In other words, over two-fifths of all citations come from six books of the Bible.

Certain Fundamentalist and Landmark confessions of the twentieth century conspicuously depart from historic statements regarding the Scripture's authority in religious matters—omitting the phrase "the rule of faith and practice" from their own confessions,[116] omitting the phrase "salvation for its end" from revisions of the New Hampshire confession,[117] relating infallibility to verbal inspiration,[118] emphasizing inerrancy,[119] contending for the literal and historical accuracy of "the Genesis account of creation,"[120] accepting at "face and full value" scriptural statements on certain aspects of Christ's earthly and post-resurrection life,[121] concentrating "on certain fundamentals of the revealed truth,"[122] and requiring full and free subscription to doctrinal propositions as a condition for certain privileges, including voting.[123]

Refusing to bow to Fundamentalist pressures in 1925, the Southern Baptist Convention inserted "religious" into its article on "the Scriptures" to make it read "religious opinions." This rules out the Fundamentalist notion that Scripture is authoritative in all areas, including history and science. The Convention also affirmed that confessions of faith, being "statements of religious convictions, drawn from the Scriptures, . . . are not to be used to hamper freedom of thought or investigation in other realms of life."[124]

To sum up: the Scripture's authority and infallibility relate to its supremacy as a rule for religious faith and practice. The official records of Baptists, prior to the twentieth century, do not claim that the Scripture's authority is dependent on its historical accuracy or that it pertains to non-religious areas. There are some individuals, however, who assert that none of the Bible can be authoritative unless all of it is inerrant. Some self-styled Bible-lovers even suggest that it should be thrown away if it has one error. Quite frankly, it is hard to understand this willingness to throw the Bible away for such slight cause. It is even harder to understand how anyone could treasure his theory about the Bible more than the Bible itself.

# VII. Threats to Scripture and Liberty of Conscience

In each generation the authority of Scripture is threatened. Throughout Christian history, the chief threats have been tradition, authoritarianism and dogma.

A perennial nemesis is tradition, which is sometimes disguised by such innocent and popular terms as general will, "grass roots" understanding and consensus. As defined over 1500 years ago, tradition is "that which has been believed everywhere, always and by all." Thus, it claims ubiquity, antiquity and unanimity. It assumes the continuity of consensus, unchanged. Its grand ideal is uniformity.

Appeals to tradition crop up in the most unlikely places, even among Baptists. Who has not heard the slogan: "All true Baptists have always believed so-and-so"? The logic—or illogic—of this slogan may be seen in a syllogism: (1) All true Baptists agree on basic doctrines. (2) We are true Baptists and understand these basic doctrines in this way. (3) Therefore, all true Baptists have understood and now understand these basic doctrines in this way. According to this popularized version of tradition, a group has only to assert its belief and then absolutize it as the historic position of all true Baptists everywhere and at all times. In a given assembly there may be as many "historic positions" as there are individuals, and they may deny any effort seeking clarification of meaning.

Consensus has no meaning in corporate life until it is defined. The history of totalitarianism, in both non-religious and religious institutions, suggests that people view with disfavor the chaotic confusion created by competing conceptions of the consensus. They want some certitude and seek it in uniformity. But someone has to define the consensus. Therefore, they took to leaders, formal or informal, to tell them what they believe. Thus, dogma, the distilled essence of tradition, is established, and authorities are empowered to enforce and guard it. The end of this process in religion, which incidentally is a recurrent theme in Christian history, is the displacement of God's authority in Scripture by man's authority in dogma.

Historically, Baptists are in that noble tradition which proclaims and protects the authority of Scripture, and its companion principles, the priesthood of the believer and liberty of conscience. For, without them, Scripture would become the property of a functional priestcraft, and an individual would have to approach God through a human mediator and read the Scripture through the eyes of dogma.

We are all familiar with the clamor for the fencing of Scripture, the priesthood of the believer and liberty of conscience by vague tradition, codified dogma and ecclesiastical authorities. Some contend that schools must be conveyors of the consensus; that all Baptists may hold and propagate whatever views they deem consistent with Scripture—except teachers, who must teach "what Baptists believe" and step to the cadence of money talk; that teaching must conform to "grass-roots" understanding.

These contentions contain dangerous implications: that schools are not really needed, for consensus can and does exist without it; that education should be indoctrination; that consensus stands at least equal or superior to Scripture and does not need to come under the judgment of Scripture; that eternal truth is coterminous with current consensus; that the progressive principle basic to our Baptist heritage —to follow God's way and truth "made known or to be made known"—is no longer permitted among Baptists; and that "grass-rootsology" is infallible and authoritative.

If consensus becomes the norm of teaching, expediency will require that teachers of religion give more attention to the human Babel than to the Holy Bible; that they take greater care to trace the blowing of the wind than the listing of the Spirit; that they base their teachings on the shifting sand of changing consensus rather than on the changeless Rock.

The exclusion of Baptist teachers from the responsible liberty which Baptists proclaim would be fraught with danger for all Baptists. Any arbitrary curtailment of a teacher's liberty to teach within the bounds of Scripture would certainly affect a student's liberty to learn. Any liberty which excludes the teacher would be a counterfeit freedom for all. This does not mean, of course, that teachers are the only interpreters of Scripture; but, it does mean that they too are interpreters, and that they merit the same freedom which others exercise and enjoy. If a teacher's liberty is only a freedom to agree with the consensus, a case could be made out for the determination of curricula, reading lists and class lectures by students. Moreover, if agreement with consensus be the grand ideal for teachers, it will become the grand ideal for every Baptist.

Am I suggesting that a teacher's liberty should have no bounds? Of course not. For the Christian teacher, academic freedom is bound by the canon, not by consensus. For each Baptist, freedom is also bound by the canon, not by consensus. Since no man is infallible, true liberty must permit the possibility of error. But error must be judged by canon, not by consensus. To be sure, one may misuse his liberty by sinning in mind, as well as in body and spirit—but teachers have no monopoly at this point. In such case, one wholly destroys "the end of Christian liberty" which is to "serve the Lord without fear in Holiness, and Righteousness."[125]

Nevertheless, God has not turned over to any person or organization, religious or otherwise, the authority to deny liberty of conscience to any or all on the grounds that some would abuse it. "God alone is Lord of the Conscience, and he has left it free from the doctrines and commandments of men which are [in any way] contrary to His Word or not contained in it."[126] It is God's "revealed will . . . for the consciences of all men to be ruled, and regulated, and guided" by the Scripture, "through the assistance of his spirit."[127]

In 1925 the committee which recommended a statement of faith to the Southern Baptist Convention was apparently concerned to defend Scripture and conscience against the encroachment of dogma, coming from a new breed of Baptists espousing an old creed of some non-Baptists calling for doctrinal uniformity. The committee recommended and the Convention adopted a five-point statement on "the historic Baptist conception of the nature and functions of confessions of faith in our religious and denominational life," on the ground that it would "clarify the atmosphere and remove some causes of misunderstanding, friction, and apprehension." Confessions are designed, the 1925 statement says, "for the general instruction and guidance" of the approving body. They "are not intended to add anything to the simple conditions of salvation revealed in the New Testament"—repentance and faith. Scripture alone "is the sole authority for faith and practice among Baptists," and "confessions are only guides in interpretation, having no authority over conscience." Being "statements of religious convictions, drawn from the Scriptures," they "are not to be used to hamper freedom of thought or investigation in other realms of life." Since confessions are not "complete statements of our faith, having any quality of finality or infallibility," Baptists "should hold themselves free to revise their statements of faith as may seem to them wise and expedient at any time."[128]

At the present time, Southern Baptists are exercising their freedom to revise and restate their faith. But this freedom to revise is also a non-absolute freedom and is to be exercised within the bounds of Scripture. To preserve the Baptist genius, this freedom must be exercised in such way as to insure that revisions are not given "any quality of finality or infallibility," to insure that revisions neither challenge the Scripture's authority nor exercise "authority over conscience."

Each generation has some who seem concerned to defend their own dogma against the encroachment of Scripture and conscience. To determine beforehand how Scripture must be studied and what it must say is to annul the supremacy of Scripture from which religious meaning still bursts forth with divine freshness; to limit the Holy Spirit, who still has the power to guide man into the ways of God, revealed in Scripture; to tyrannize over individual consciences which still yearn for freedom in Christ; and to compel uniformity—all of which are contrary to our historic position.

The dictatorship of dogma sterilizes one against thinking and enslaves his spirit as well as his mind. It is to be feared. Much to be prized, however, is the tyranny of divine truth which makes one a slave *only* to the sacred duty of studying the Scripture with open mind and spirit, to the end that he may learn for himself and communicate to others the Son of God, who is truth in its fullest religious sense, and the One—the only One—in whom we find freedom.

## Notes

[1]Except where otherwise noted, all quotations from Baptist confessions in this article will be taken from William L. Lumpkin, *Baptist Confessions Of Faith* (Philadelphia: The Judson Press, 1959). They will be identified by "Lumpkin" and the page number.

[2]Myles Coverdale's *The Bible* (1535): "that is, the holy scripture of the Olde and New Testament, faithfully and truly translated out of Douche and Latyn into Englishe"; Thomas Matthew's *The Byble* (1537): "which is all the holy Scripture: in which are contayned the Olde and Newe Testament, truly and purely translated into Englysh"; the great Bible (1539): "*The Byble in Englyshe*, that is to saye the content of all the holy scripture, both of the olde and newe testament, truly translated after the verytye of the Hebrue and Greke textes, by the dylygent studye of dyuerse excellent learned men, expert in the foresayde tonges"; and the Geneva Bible (1560): "The Bible and Holy Scriptures, Conteyned in the Olde and

Newe testament. Translated according to the Ebrue and Greke, and conferred with the best translations in divers languages."

[3]The title of the Authorized Version (KJV) reads: "The Holy Bible, Conteyning the Old Testament and the New: Newly Translated out of the Originall tongues, with the former Translations diligently compared and revised, by his Majesties speciall commandement. Appointed to be read in Churches. Imprinted at London by Robert Barker, Printer to the Kings most Excellent Majestie. Anno Dom. 1611."

[4]*The Baptist Catechism* (1794) 9. 5.

[5]Art. i, Lumpkin, 361. Incidentally, this is the first use of the phrase, "Holy Bible," in a Baptist confession.

[6]Chap. i, Lumpkin, 248.    [7]Art. xxxvii, Lumpkin, 324f.

[8]Lumpkin, 245f.    [9]Art. 3, Lumpkin, 103.

[10]Art. 1, Lumpkin, 117; cf. art. vii, 227 and art. iii, 299, which add "and these three are one." These are General Baptist confessions.

[11]Art. 12, Lumpkin, 120.    [12]Art. 31, Lumpkin, 129.

[13]Art. 2nd, Lumpkin, 198.    [14]Art. ii, Lumpkin, 204.

[15]Chap. ii, art. 3, Lumpkin, 253.    [16]Art. iv, Lumpkin, 299.

[17]Art. xxxi, Lumpkin, 320.    [18]Art. xxiv, Lumpkin, 163.

[19]Art. 58, Lumpkin, 135.    [20]Arts 73f., Lumpkin, 137f.

[21]See Bromiley's introduction and translation in the *Library of Christian Classics*, vol. xxiv, 51-95.

[22]Art. viii, Lumpkin, 158; chap, i, art. 2, 249.

[23]Art. 2, Lumpkin, 355; art. ii, 358; art. 1st, 359; art 1, 383.

[24]Art. 1, Lumpkin, 383; art, i.1, 385.    [25]Art. 23, Lumpkin, 122.

[26]Art. i.1, Lumpkin, 385.    [27]Southern Baptist Convention *Annual* (1962) item 57.

[28]Chap. 1, art. 5, Lumpkin, 250.

[29]Southern Baptist Convention *Annual* (1951) 61.

[30]Art. 46, Lumpkin, 182.    [31]Art. 3rd, Lumpkin, 198; chap. i, art. 2, 249.

[32]Art. xxi, Lumpkin, 209.

[33]Chap. i, art. 4, Lumpkin, 250; cf. art. i, 361; art. 1, 393.

[34]Chap. i, art. 10, Lumpkin, 252.    [35]Chap. i, art. 3, Lumpkin, 249.

[36]Art. 35, Lumpkin, 112.    [37]Art. 37, Lumpkin, 64.

[38]Art. xviii, Lumpkin, 207.    [39]Art. i, Lumpkin, 361.

[40]Art. 1, Lumpkin, 378.    [41]Art. 2, Lumpkin, 380.    [42]Art. 1, Lumpkin, 385.

[43]Art. i, Lumpkin, 361f.; art. 1, 393. [44]Chap. i, art. 8, Lumpkin, 251.

[45]Quoted by Heinrich Heppe, *Reformed Dogmatics*, 17.    [46]*Ibid.*, 19f.

[47]Thomas Grantham, *Christianismus Primitivus*, vol. i, 2f.    [48]*Ibid.*, vol. i, 5.

[49]Art. 46, Lumpkin, 182; art. xxi, 209.    [50]Chap. i, art. 1, Lumpkin, 248f.

[51]Art. xxxvii, Lumpkin, 325.

[52]Southern Baptist Convention *Annual* (1946) "Statement of Principles," 38f.

[53]Clifton J. Allen and W. L. Howse, eds., *Curriculum Guide* (Nashville TN: Convention Press, 1961) 7.

[54]Art. xx, Lumpkin, 55.    [55]Art. xix, Lumpkin, 54.    [56]Art. 19, Lumpkin, 107.

[57]Art. 68, Lumpkin, 136.    [58]Art. vi, Lumpkin, 226.    [59]*Cf. supra*, n. 56.

[60]Art. xxiii, Lumpkin, 314. [61]Art. xxii, Lumpkin, 162f.

[62]Chap. xiv, art. 2, Lumpkin, 268f. [63]Art. viii, Lumpkin, 364.

[64]*Abstract of Principles*, Southern Baptist Theological Seminary, art. 10.

[65]Art. 3, Lumpkin, 378.　　[66]Art. xviii, Lumpkin, 389.

[67]Art. 19, Lumpkin, 107; art. 68, 136; art. vi, 226; art. xxiii, 314.

[68]Art. xxiii, Lumpkin, 162f.; chap. xiv, art. 2, 268f.

[69]Chap. i, art. 6, Lumpkin, 250.　　[70]Chap. i, art. 9, Lumpkin, 251.f.

[71]*Cf. supra*, n. 51. [72]*Cf. supra*, n. 70. [73]*Cf. supra*, n. 69.

[74]*Cf. supra*, n. 51. [75]*A Glimpse of Sions Glory* (1641), 13f.

[76]*Cf. supra*, n. 69. [77]*Cf. supra*, n. 39. [78]Chap. i, art. 7, Lumpkin, 251.

[79]Art. v, Lumpkin, 386.　　[80]*Cf. supra*, n. 66. [81]*Cf. supra*, n. 78.

[82]Chap. 1, arts. 4f., Lumpkin, 250. [83]*Cf. supra*, n. 4. [84]*Cf. supra*, n. 56.

[85]Art. viii, Lumpkin, 158. [86]*Cf. supra*, n. 78. [87]Art. 2, Lumpkin, 355.

[88]*Cf. supra*, n. 51. [89]*Cf. supra*, n. 69. [90]Art. 3d, Lumpkin, 198.

[91]Chap. i, Lumpkin, 369.　　[92]Art. i, Lumpkin, 361; art. 1, 393.

[93]*Cf. supra*, n. 56. [94]*Cf. supra*, n. 39.

[95]Art. viii, Lumpkin, 158; *cf.* Southern Seminary's *Abstract of Principles*, art. 10.

[96]Art. xxii, Lumpkin, 163; chap. xiv, art. 2, 269.

[97]Arts. 4, 5 and 7, Lumpkin, 125.

[98]Art. 1, Lumpkin, 102; art, iii, 225; art. i, 156; art. 1st, 198; chap. ii, 252f.; art. i, 298; chap. ii, 369.

[99]Quoted in Lumpkin, 191.　　[100]*Cf. supra*, n. 38.

[101]Art. xxiii, Lumpkin, 232.　　[102]Art. xxvi, 316. [103]*Cf. supra*, n. 90.

[104]Chap. i, art. 2, Lumpkin, 249.　　[105]Art. ii, Lumpkin, 358; art. 1st, 359.

[106]Art. B.1, Lumpkin, 345. [107]*The Baptist Catechism* (1794) q.4.

[108]No. 4, Lumpkin, 392.

[109]Art. vii, Lumpkin, 158; *cf.* chap. xxii, art. 7, 282.

[110]Chap. xxvi, art. 5, Lumpkin, 286.　　[111]Art. i, Lumpkin, 362; art. i, 393.

[112]*Cf. supra*, n. 69.　　[113]*Cf.* chap. i, art. 10, Lumpkin, 252; art, xxxvii, 325; 191.

[114]*Cf. supra* n. 111.　　[115]Art. 27, Lumpkin, 109; *cf.* art. xxix, 59.

[116]Art. 1, Lumpkin, 378; art. 2, 380. [117]Art. 1, Lumpkin, 383; art. i, 385.

[118]*Cf. supra*, n. 116.　　[119]Art. i.2, Lumpkin, 385.

[120]Art. v, Lumpkin, 386; art. 3, 378; art. 3, 380.

[121]Art. xviii, Lumpkin, 389; *cf.* arts. 7f. 378f.; arts. 8, 15 and 22, 380.

[122]Lumpkin, 378. [123]Lumpkin, 382. [124]No. 5, Lumpkin, 392.

[125]Chap. xxi, art. 3, Lumpkin, 280.

[126]Art. 18, Lumpkin, 396; *cf.* chap. xxi, art. 2, 279f.; art. xlvi, 331f.

[127]Art. xlvi, 331f. [128]Lumpkin, 392.

# Biographical Notes

**Elizabeth Barnes** is Professor of Theology and Ethics, Baptist Theological Seminary, Richmond, Virginia.

**George R. Beasley-Murray** is Senior Professor of New Testament Interpretation, The Southern Baptist Theological Seminary, Louisville, Kentucky.

**Hardy Clemons** is Pastor, First Baptist Church, Greenville, South Carolina, and Moderator (1993–1994) of the Cooperative Baptist Fellowship.

**Ralph H. Elliott** is Retired Vice President for Academic Life and Dean of the Faculty, Colgate Rochester/Bexley Hall/Crozer Theological Seminary, Rochester, New York and former pastor of several American Baptist churches.

**Clyde E. Fant** is Dean of the Chapel and O. L. Walker Professor of Christian Studies, Stetson University, DeLand, Florida.

**Paul S. Fiddes** is Principal, Regent's Park College, University of Oxford, Oxford, England.

**E. Glenn Hinson** is Professor of Spirituality, Worship, and Church History at the Baptist Theological Seminary, Richmond, Virginia.

**William E. Hull** is Provost, Samford University, Birmingham, Alabama.

**Fisher Humphreys** is Professor of Theology, Beeson Divinity School, Samford University, Birmingham, Alabama.

**Charles E. Poole** is Pastor, First Baptist Church, Macon, Georgia.

**Robert B. Setzer, Jr.** is Pastor, First Baptist Church, Danville, Virginia.

**H. Stephen Shoemaker** is Pastor, Broadway Baptist Church, Ft. Worth, Texas.

**Walter B. Shurden** is editor of the series *Proclaiming the Baptist Vision* and Callaway Professor and Chair, Department of Christianity, Mercer University, Macon, Georgia.

**Karen E. Smith** is Lecturer, South Wales Baptist College and University of Wales, College of Cardiff, and Minister, Orchard Place Baptist Church, Neath, Wales.

**R. Wayne Stacy** is Senior Minister, First Baptist Church, Raleigh North Carolina.

**Frank Stagg** is Professor Emeritus of New Testament Interpretation, The Southern Baptist Theological Seminary, Louisville, Kentucky.

**Hugh Wamble** was Professor of Church History at the Midwestern Baptist Theological Seminary in Kansas City, Missouri.